The Fulfilled Family

by
John MacArthur, Jr.

WORD OF GRACE COMMUNICATIONS
P.O. Box 4000
Panorama City, CA 91412

Moody Press Edition, 1987

Library of Congress Cataloging in Publication Data

MacArthur, John F.
    The fulfilled family.

    (Bible studies)
    Includes index.
    1. Marriage—Biblical teaching.   2. Family—Biblical
teaching.   3. Bible.   N.T.   Ephesians V, 21-VI, 4 —
Criticism, interpretation, etc.   I. Title.   II. Series:
MacArthur, John F.   Bible studies.
BS2655.M34M33   1987   248.4   86-31277
ISBN 0-8024-5318-X

1 2 3 4 5 6 7 Printing/LC/Year 91 90 89 88 87

Contents

1
The Divine Pattern for Marriage—Part 1
The Necessary Foundation

Outline

Introduction
A. The Peril of Marriage and Family
B. The Preservation of Marriage and Family
    1. The priority
    2. The presupposition
    3. The power

Lesson
I. The Spirit-Filled Relationship (v. 21)
    A. Submission Explained
    B. Submission Exemplified
    C. Submission Examined
        1. The principle of mutual submission
          a) Illustrated in the family
          b) Illustrated in the marriage relationship
        2. The principle of authority and submission
          a) In the Godhead
          b) In marriage
          c) In government
          d) In the family
          e) In the church

Introduction

A. The Peril of Marriage and Family

Our generation is watching the death of marriage and the family as we know it. Among the many factors contributing to its destruction are immorality, adultery, fornication, homosexuality, abortion, sterilization, women's liberation, delinquency, and sexual rebellion. All those things are like strands in a cord that is strangling the family.

There are many opinions about the restructuring of the family. Some sociologists say marriages need to change. They say we need "open marriages" or "non-marriages" and that it really doesn't matter whether marriages continue as they have in the past. People are groping, without any base of authority, to try to find out how to make meaningful relationships in a disintegrating society.

B. The Preservation of Marriage and Family

It's time for Christians to reiterate the divine pattern. Our marriages and families should demonstrate a way of living that is rewarding, meaningful, and fulfilling. That divine pattern should be evident to the world as it looks at Christian marriages and families. Unfortunately, the world's problem of divorce has also become a problem of the church. But God has the divine standard that can make marriage and the family what they ought to be.

1. The priority

It we don't preserve the family, society will crumble. The family is the basic building block of society. When it goes, everything goes. The ability to pass on meaningful advice to the next generation is lost when there is no communication and discipline. Every society becomes an end in itself, and those who are loudest and most vocal will dominate.

2. The presupposition

Before you can know the divine pattern that can make your marriage and family life meaningful, you must meet one requirement: you must be a Christian. The book of Ephesians, which discusses the divine pattern, is written to believers. If you're not a believer, there is little hope that you can make your marriage and family anything near what God intends it to be. Now I'm not saying that nonbelievers can't have meaningful relationships. They can—but only up to a point. They will never know total fulfillment. As an individual can find fulfillment only in a relationship with God, a family can find fulfillment only if its definition is designed and authored by God Himself. So, apart from knowing Jesus Christ, we can't expect a family to be fulfilled, because God is the One who created man, invented marriage and the family, and wrote the book on how marriage is to function.

3. The power

There's more to having a meaningful and fulfilled marriage and family than just being a believer. There are many Christians who know and love the Lord who are not living according to His moral, marital, or familial laws. Why? Because they are not filled with the Spirit. It's one thing to possess the Spirit of God and another to be filled by Him. Ephesians 5:18 says, "Be not drunk with wine, in which is excess, but be filled with the Spirit." In other words, every Christian possesses the Spirit but is not always controlled by, or filled with, the Spirit. And when we're not controlled by the Spirit of God, our family life will manifest that. A carnal believer is going to have discord in his family because he has discord between himself and God. So, to be a believer is the starting point; but being controlled with the Spirit is what brings results.

We're drowning in a sea of information on marriage today: marriage seminars, marriage conferences, marriage encounters, marriage books, and marriage counselors. People think the first thing to do when they have a marital problem is to see a counselor, psychiatrist, or analyst, buy a supply of books, go to a seminar, listen to tapes, or fill out charts. I don't want to oversimplify this, but if you're not filled with the Spirit, you can do all those things, but none of them will matter. On the other hand, if you're filled with the Spirit, He'll control your relationships. Now counseling, books, and seminars can be helpful in giving you practical hints on how being filled with the Spirit should work itself out in your relationships, but the epitome of the Christian life is to be filled and controlled by the Holy Spirit. Only when that happens will our families be what God wants them to be. That is what Paul is saying in the passage beginning in Ephesians 5:18.

Lesson

I. The Spirit-Filled Relationship (v. 21)

Ephesians 5:21 says, "Submitting yourselves one to another in the fear of God." When we genuinely reverence, fear, and worship God, we submit to one another. Submission is vital in the church. James 4:1 says, "What is the source of quarrels and conflicts among you? Is not the source your pleasures that wage war in your members?" (NASB*). Conflicts in the church arise because people want their rights, they want their way, they want to lead the group, and they want their opinion to dominate, so they push their way to the top. But someone who is Spirit-filled doesn't fight for the top; he fights for the bottom. Throughout Scripture we are called to submit (1 Cor. 16:16; 1 Pet. 2:13; 5:5; Heb. 13:17).

A. Submission Explained

The word *submit* is from the Greek word *hupotassō* (*hupo*, "under"; *tasso*, "to line up," "to get in order," "to arrange"), which, in a military sense, means "to rank beneath or under." As Christians, we are to rank ourselves under one another, not over one another. The whole mentality of the Christian life as we relate to each other is one of humility and submissiveness.

B. Submission Exemplified

Philippians 2:4-8 says, "Look not every man on his own things, but every man also on the things of others. Let this mind be in you, which was also in Christ Jesus, who, being in the form of God, thought it not robbery to be equal with God, but made himself of no reputation, and took upon him the form of a servant, and was made in the likeness of

New American Standard Bible.

10

men; and, being found in fashion as a man, he humbled himself and became obedient unto death, even the death of the cross."

C. Submission Examined

1. The principle of mutual submission

In our relationships we are to be submissive. That is a general principle for all believers to follow. Now, in terms of structure and function, there is to be authority and submission; but in terms of interpersonal relationships, there is to be mutual submission. The principle of authority and submission is in the church, in the government, and in the home; but that doesn't change the fact that we are to mutually submit to one other. It's mutual submission the apostle Paul is after in Ephesians 5:22–6:9. Paul uses the family to illustrate the concept, starting in verse 21.

Note that wives receive the brunt of this section in Ephesians 5. I'm sure the statement of verse 22, "Wives, submit yourselves unto your own husbands," is etched in granite in many homes. There's a tendency for men to grab their wives and yell, "Submit!" But did you know that the verb *submit* does not appear in the original manuscript in verse 22? It's only implied from verse 21. What is Paul saying then? He is saying everyone is to submit to everyone else—and he shows us how from the family.

a) Illustrated in the family

In verse 22, wives are to submit to their husbands; but in verse 25, husbands are to submit to their wives. You may ask, "In what way?" Verse 25 says, "Husbands, love your wives, even as Christ also loved the church, and gave himself for it." I don't know of any greater act of submission than to die for someone—and that's the way husbands are to treat their wives. A husband is to submit to his wife, not in the sense of abdicating his responsibility of leadership, but in the sense of getting under her to bear her

11

burdens, carry her cares, meet her needs, and sacrifice his own desires to fulfill her needs.

In Ephesians 6:1-3, children are to submit in obedience to their parents; but in verse 4, parents also are to submit (the word *fathers* in verse 4 could be broadened to mean "parents"). Parents are to submit to their children in the sense that they are not to provoke them to wrath but instead "bring them up in the nurture and admonition of the Lord."

We are all to submit. A servant needs to submit to his master (vv. 5-8), but a master needs to submit by never doing wrong to that servant (v. 9). We all have to submit. Every relationship in the family illustrates mutual submissiveness. We need to keep that in mind. Remember, Paul was talking to the whole church when he said, "We are all to submit to one another" (v. 21).

b) Illustrated in the marriage relationship

Even though there is authority and submission in the marriage relationship, there is also a beautiful mutuality. First Corinthians 7:3 says, "Let the husband render unto the wife her due." The husband has a submissive part to play in that he is to submit and render to his wife what she needs. However, verse 3 continues, "And likewise also, the wife unto the husband." Verse 4 says, "The wife hath not the power of her own body, but the husband; and likewise also the husband hath not power of his own body, but the wife." That is mutuality. It does not negate the leadership responsibility, but it recognizes the mutual submissiveness that must occur in a marriage and a family at every point. It is the basic principle of family life.

2. The principle of authority and submission

Even though we are all equal in the sight of God according to Galatians 3:28, authority and submission must be present in terms of function. That is illustrated in many ways.

12

a) In the Godhead

In 1 Corinthians 11:3 Paul says, "I would have you know that the head of every man is Christ; and the head of the woman is the man; and the head of Christ is God." You may ask, "Does that mean God is the head over Christ? I thought They were one." Jesus said, "He that hath seen me hath seen the Father" (John 14:9), and, "I and my Father are one" (John 10:30). John 1:1 says that the Word (Christ) was face-to-face (Gk., *pros ton theon*) with God. Hebrews 1 says that Christ was exalted to be equal with God. What does it mean that God is the head of Christ? God's headship over Christ is not a matter of essence; it is a matter of function. Within the function of the Godhead, it was deemed necessary that Christ submit Himself. The same Jesus who said, "All authority is given unto me in heaven and in earth" (Matt. 28:18) also said, "My food is to do the will of him that sent me" (John 4:34). In essence and nature, Christ and God are the same; but by God's design, the function of the Son demanded that He submit to the Father in a beautiful act of humiliation.

b) In marriage

The same is true in marriage. The essence, the spiritual quality, and the position before God of both husband and wife are the same; but in the family, for the sake of function, the woman is to take the place of submission to the leadership of man. God has made the man stronger, capable of harder physical labor, and has given him the responsibility of taking the brunt of difficult circumstances. The wife's tenderness and gentleness, then, are to support and balance the husband's strength. The point is that there is mutual submission in marriage, but it doesn't negate the principle of authority and submission.

c) In government

In government we have both authority and submission. Now those in authority are not necessarily godly people. You may ask, "Why aren't the spiritual leaders the ones in authority in the government?" Romans 13:1 says "the powers that be are ordained of God." It's God's responsibility to deal with that, not ours. Verse 4 says God has given authority to policemen, soldiers, and other government agents. Peter said we are to submit to every ordinance (law) of man, to the king, to the governors, and to everyone in authority over us (1 Pet. 2:13-18). Why? Because God knows society is maintained on the basis of authority and submission. It doesn't mean there is a spiritual, intellectual, or essential inequality; God is simply talking about function.

The largest unit of relationships is the government. And according to Romans 13 and 1 Peter 2, nations must function with authority. On the one hand, there will be rulers, kings, governors, policemen, soldiers, and leaders; and on the other hand there will be those who follow their leadership. Why? Because they are better than everyone else? No; because there has to be authority and submission or there will be anarchy, and no society can survive anarchy.

d) In the family

In the smallest unit of relationships, the family, the same principle holds true. You cannot have anarchy in a family, with no one responsible for discipline, for earning wages, for controlling behavior, or for giving direction. That would bring nothing but chaos. Unfortunately, that is precisely what is happening in America today. The dissolution of the family is the beginning of the dissolution of the nation—the beginning of anarchy. If we have anarchy in the family now, we will soon have anarchy in the nation, and then we will see the death of American society. Mankind cannot function apart from the principle of authority and submission. It's not a matter of who's better—it's just that God made it that way to preserve society.

e) In the church

We also have to have authority and submission in the church. Men are to preach in the church. Why? Because that is how God designed it. In 1 Timothy 2:11, Paul says this in reference to when the church comes together: "Let the women learn in silence with all subjection." There is no allowance in the Bible for women preachers. Further, in verse 12 Paul says, "I permit not a woman to teach, nor to usurp authority over the man, but to be in silence." That is the standard for the church. Now does that mean women are inferior? Of course not! The Old Testament as well as the New shows us many examples of godly women. Women have touched the globe in a way that men never could, framing and forming society. But there has to be some order in the church, so God has designed men to be the strength, the force, and the leadership of the church.

In 1 Timothy 2:13-14 Paul tells us that the submissive role of women is designed by the order of creation, "for Adam was first formed, then Eve," and affirmed by a judicial act of God because "Adam was not deceived, but the woman, being deceived, was in the transgression." However, Paul gives a beautiful balance in verse 15: "Notwithstanding, she shall be saved in childbearing." The woman needs to submit to the leadership of the man in the family and church, but she doesn't have a second-class role. She is able to bear, nurse, love, and influence children in a way that a father never can.

So, while there is equality, mutuality, and a beautiful balance in the family, there is still authority and submission. We're going to see as we go through this passage (5:22–6:4) that we are *all* to submit; yet that in no way negates the fact that God has also designed a tremendous authority-submission principle to function in the family.

Today's Marriages and Their Effect on the Next Generation

I'm concerned about today's marriages. Each year several million couples pledge themselves in marriage, vowing to love each other for better or worse. But about half of those marriages will end in divorce. That contributes to the problem of unwanted children. There are as many abortions by married women as non-married. Couples often don't want children. One-third of all couples in their child-bearing years have been sterilized. Why? Because children interfere with divorce. If you don't have children, you can leave easier. Children get in the way.

We have a generation of children growing up in families that are in chaos. Many children are saying to themselves, *The last thing I want to do is get married. I don't want to repeat this mess.* They've lived in chaotic and totally unfulfilled families, so they don't want anything to do with marriage. But they want to fulfill their sex drives, so they go from person to person with no commitment. The next generation may never get married.

Even marriages that do hang together are often characterized by adultery, unfaithfulness, lying, cheating, loss of respect, loss of trust, pride, self-centeredness, materialism, laziness, and loneliness. Our nation is a mess, but the sad thing is that those characteristics have crept into the church. Believers are having marital problems, too. The answer is not more counselors, more marriage seminars, or more books on marriage; the answer is in Ephesians 5:18: "Be filled with the Holy Spirit." When that is accomplished, God Himself will produce the virtues that make for a meaningful marriage. People are good at patching up symptoms but not so good at dealing with reality. What we need to do is back up and look at God's principles.

The Condition of Marriage in Paul's Day

When Paul began to preach about the divine standards for marriage, the situation was much the same as it is today.

1. The Jews

   The Jews had developed a low view of women. To them, women were servants. In fact, when a Jewish man would get up in the morning, he would pray, "God, I thank You that I'm not a Gentile, a slave, or a woman. Amen." In Deuteronomy 24:1 Moses says that if a husband found uncleanness in his wife, he could divorce her. Some rabbis interpreted "uncleanness" as adultery and said that was the only grounds for divorce. But others said that "uncleanness" could be anything from spoiling the dinner to not being as pretty as another woman. Basically the two views among the rabbis about the proper grounds for divorce were: (1) adultery only; and (2) for any reason at all. When those two choices were offered to the people, which do you think they accepted? By the time of Jesus and Paul, the Jews were divorcing their wives on whim.

2. The Greeks

The Greeks were worse than the Jews. In the Greek world, there wasn't a legal procedure for divorce, because it wasn't necessary. Wives only cleaned the house and had legitimate children. Demosthenes, an Athenian orator and statesman, said, "We have courtesans for the sake of pleasure; we have concubines for the sake of daily cohabitation; and we have wives for the purpose of having children legitimately and being faithful guardians for our household affairs." Because Greek men found their pleasures outside of marriage, fornication and prostitution were rampant. And according to historians, Athenian society was also dominated by homosexuality, lesbianism, and pedophilia (the sexual abuse of children).

3. The Romans

The Romans were even worse than the Greeks. Divorce was not the exception but the norm. Jerome, an ancient writer, tells of one Roman woman who married her twenty-third husband —and she was his twenty-first wife! Marriage in Rome became nothing more than legalized prostitution. In other words, you could get married when you found someone you wanted, stay until you got tired of her, dump her, and then marry someone else. Rome also had a rampant women's liberation movement. Women didn't want to have children because they thought it hurt their looks. Woman wanted to do everything men did, so there were women wrestlers and women fencers. According to Juvenal, the first- and second-century Roman satirical poet, women joined in men's hunts "with spear in hand and breasts exposed, and took to pig-sticking." Then he went on to write,

"What modesty can you expect in a woman who wears a helmet, abjures her own sex, and delights in the feats of strength?" (*Satires* 1.22-23, 61-62; 6.246-64).

That was the condition of marriage when Paul wrote: "Wives, submit yourselves unto your own husbands, as unto the Lord. . . . Husbands, love your wives, even as Christ also loved the church" (Eph. 5:22, 25). He was not saying, "Now, I just want to remind you of what you already know." He was calling them to a new standard of living. He was telling them to live in a way they knew nothing about.

The Song of Solomon: A Look at God-Designed Marriage

While authority and submission is to exist in the home, our relationships should be bathed in love so that they melt together with mutual love and respect. This is illustrated in the Song of Solomon, where we will see a beautiful picture of a right marriage relationship. It is a beautiful example of how leadership is to work.

1. The perspective

   In 2:3-15, the Shulamite woman acknowledges her husband as the head of the home. She saw him as her protector (v. 3), her provider (v. 4), her sustainer (v. 5), her security (v. 6), and her leader and initiator (vv. 10-15). There is no oppression or dictatorial spirit in this passage. She desired his leadership, and he took the role that God had given him. Now, even though authority and submission are present, verse 10 describes a beautiful mutuality: "My beloved is mine, and I am his" (cf. 7:10).

2. The portrait

   In 5:10-16, we see a marvelous portrait of the Shulamite woman's husband through her eyes of love. She saw him as handsome (v. 10) and bronzed (v. 11), with soft, tender, misty eyes (v. 12). There was color in his cheeks (v. 13), his lips were fragrant (v. 13), his hands were bronzed (v. 14), and his stomach and legs were muscular and strong (vv. 14-15). She saw him as a strong, handsome, rugged character. In verse 16, when he opens his mouth, he isn't crass or rude. Then at the end of verse 16 she says, "This is my beloved, and this is my friend." She didn't see him as a dictator; she saw him as a beloved friend. The mutuality and the spirit of love fits beautifully with authority and submission when love bathes the relationship.

3. The problem

Now you may say, "If my husband or wife was like that, we'd never have a problem." But in chapter 5, we find that this couple did have a problem—the wife would not submit to her husband. In verse 1 the husband comes home late at night, after his wife is already in bed. He was full of love for her, and he knocked on the door, asking that she let him in (v. 2). Her response to him, however, was basically, "Don't bother me now; I'm asleep. I'm not interested" (v. 3). But when she heard his hand on the door, love welled up in her heart, and she felt sorry for her lack of submissiveness (v. 4). So, she got up, put her robe on, and opened the door (v. 5). Unfortunately, it was too late—he had already gone (v. 6).

Note that he was submissive to her, in that he didn't force himself on her. She panicked and ran all over the city trying to find him (vv. 6-9; 6:1). Finally, she decided he was in the garden (v. 2) and found him there (v. 4). When she found him, he didn't say, "Where have you been? Why didn't you let me in?" Instead, he said some of the same things he had said to her on their wedding night (vv. 5-7; cf. 4:1-3). In confirming his love for her, he told her that even though she had rejected him, he still loved her as much as he did the night he married her. The problem was solved, and they had a wonderful time renewing their relationship (chap. 7).

The Bible has two important things to say about having a meaningful relationship: (1) we are all to mutually submit to each other; and (2) functionally, we must have authority and submission. When we learn the meaning of those two dimensions of truth, our families will be what God wants them to be.

1. What are some of the things that are contributing to the death of marriage and the family (see pp. 7-8)?
2. Although the divine pattern should be evident to the world as it looks at Christian marriages and families, why isn't it (see p. 8)?
3. What is the basic building block of human society? What happens when that building block is weakened? Why (see p. 8)?
4. What is required before a person can make his marriage and family what God intends them to be? Explain (see pp. 8-9).
5. How can believers be empowered to have meaningful and fulfilled marriages and families (see pp. 9-10)?
6. Why do conflicts arise in the church? For what position does a Spirit-filled person fight (see p. 10)?
7. Identify and explain the supreme example of submission (Phil. 2:4-8; see pp. 10-11).
8. Although there must be a balance of authority and submission in a society, what type of submission was Paul referring to in Ephesians 5:21 (see p. 11)?
9. How are husbands supposed to submit to their wives? In what sense are parents to submit to their children (see pp. 11-12)?
10. Even though all believers are of equivalent worth in the sight of God (Gal. 3:28), what must be present in terms of function (see p. 12)?
11. Explain how God can be the head of Christ when Christ is the same as the Father in essence and nature (1 Cor. 11:3; see p. 13).
12. How is the principle of authority and submission supposed to operate in a marriage? What general qualities designed by God does each partner contribute (see p. 13)?
13. Although a government may not be godly, why does the New Testament instruct Christians to submit to the government in general (see pp. 13-14)?
14. Without the principle of authority and submission in operation, to what will a society degenerate (see p. 14)?
15. How is the dissolution of the family related to the dissolution of a nation (see p. 14)?
16. What two events confirm the submissive role of women in the church (1 Tim. 2:13-14; see p. 15)?
17. Explain why a woman doesn't have a second-class role in the family and the church (see p. 15).

18. Why is there concern about the state of marriages today (see p. 16)?
19. What is the answer to the marital problems that Christians are having (see p. 16)?
20. Describe the condition of marriage among the Jews, Greeks, and Romans in Paul's day (see pp. 16-18).
21. How did the Shulamite woman acknowledge her husband in Song of Solomon? How did he demonstrate his submissiveness to her (see pp. 18-19)?

Pondering the Principles

1. To whom are believers called to submit in Ephesians 5:21, Hebrews 13:17, and 1 Peter 2:13? Are you submissive in each of those areas? In which area are you least submissive? Why? What steps do you need to take to help you become more submissive? Meditate on Philippians 2:3-8.

2. Some couples choose not to have children so they can remain independent and avoid the responsibility of raising children. They see children as a financial burden rather than a rewarding investment that yields present dividends of joy and personal growth. Read Psalm 127:3-5. If you have children, how are you treating your "gifts" from the Lord (v. 3a)? Do you acknowledge them as rewards that must be treasured (v. 3b)? Do you benefit from their usefulness (v. 4)? How have your children blessed you? Have you told them how thankful you are that God has given them to you? Take every opportunity to allow the children of unsaved neighbors to interact with your household. Let them see the harmony that is nurtured in a family committed to biblical principles.

2
The Divine Pattern for Marriage—Part 2
The Role of the Wife

Outline

Lesson
I. The Duty of the Wife (vv. 22-24)
   A. The Matter of Submission (v. 22*a*)
      1. Colossians 3:18
      2. 1 Peter 3:1-6
      3. 1 Corinthians 11:3-12
      4. Titus 2:3-5
      5. Proverbs 31:10-31
   B. The Manner of Submission (v. 22*b*)
   C. The Motive of Submission (v. 23*a*)
   D. The Model of Submission (vv. 23*b*-24)

Lesson

I. THE DUTY OF THE WIFE (vv. 22-24)

A. The Matter of Submission (v. 22*a*)

"Wives, submit yourselves unto your own husbands."

We have already seen that the Greek word for "submit"
(Gk., *hupotassō*) is not in the original text of verse 22 but is
implied from its usage in verse 21. *Hupotassō* refers to a
functional lining up and in no way implies a difference in
essence. Also, note that Paul does not use the word *obey*
(Gk., *hupakouō*) in reference to the wife. *Hupakouō*, which
means "to answer," "to attend," or "to obey," is used for

children and slaves but not for wives (Eph. 6:1, 5). A wife is not a slave, awaiting commands such as: "Do this! Get that! Go over there! Fix me that! Is my so-and-so done?" She is not a slave. The relationship between a husband and wife is much more intimate, more personal, more inward, and more vital than that. That is indicated by the phrase "your own husband." There is a possessiveness there that assumes a wife would absolutely and willingly respond in submission to her own husband—one whom she possesses. It is not a reference to inferiority; it's simply a God-ordained distinction in function so that society can be preserved.

God ordains a distinction of function in Genesis 3:16, where He says, "Thy desire shall be to thy husband, and he shall rule over thee." Yet in Genesis 2:24 God also says that the two would be one flesh. While there is an intimate, inward vitality that makes the two one, it does not violate the function of authority and submission. For the sake of unity and workability, the woman is to be subject to the leadership of her husband—not as a slave but as one who is provided for, cared for, and secured by her husband. It does not have nearly as much to do with what she does for him as what he is responsible to do for her.

Leadership belongs to the man. God designed him to be stronger physically so that he would be able to work for, protect, provide for, and give security to his wife, whom the Holy Spirit calls "the weaker vessel" (1 Pet. 3:7). Man is constituted to be the stronger partner. Someone has to be the protector—the one who provides, preserves, and cares —and from the beginning God intended that it be the man.

1. Colossians 3:18

In Colossians 3:18, a parallel passage to Ephesians 5:22, Paul writes, "Wives, submit yourselves unto your own husbands, as it is fit in the Lord." The phrase "as it is fit" or, literally, "as it is fitting" is the Greek verb *anēkō*. This verb means "to be fitting, seemly, and proper." In the Septuagint (the Greek translation of the Old Testament), *anēkō* is used of something that is legally binding. In Philemon 8 it is also used in this legal sense. What

Paul is saying, then, is this: the submission of the wife to her husband is legally binding—it's the accepted law of society.

Where does a society get its laws? When a society acknowledges any part of God's laws as its own, its laws became a reiteration of divine principles. We're quickly seeing the destruction of that concept in our society because we are now legislating morality by majority vote. But if we look back, we will find that the laws governing societies in which God has any influence, such as Western culture, came from a biblical base. For example, we have laws against murder, theft, sexual evil, and perjury. Where do those laws come from? From the Ten Commandments in Exodus 20. We have made laws commensurate with God's divine revelation. So, for the wife to submit to her husband is fitting and proper, not only because it fits the created order of God, but because man has assumed its legally binding design as well.

Have You Been Victimized by the World's View of Equal Rights?

I recognize that the issue of authority and submission in the home is not popular. But do you know why? Because we've been brainwashed. If you have trouble accepting these principles, it's because you are a part of a society that has been victimized by a godless, Christless, non-biblical philosophy of living perpetrated through the centuries.

What we're seeing in our society today was also true of the philosphy behind the French Revolution, which was a humanistic, egalitarian approach to life. The French believed they could have a society with absolute equality—a classless, godless type of humanistic existence. That idea has been brewing for years. It is now coming to full brew, and our age is drinking it in: no classes, no sexes, no distinctions, no authority, no submission, and no humility. Our society has become victimized by this atheistic approach to life. And the church, instead of rejecting it, falls right into it by supporting equal rights for homosexuals, advocating women elders and woman preachers, and functioning on philosophical, godless hermeneutics that would rather reinterpret the Bible in terms of our present time than accept the authority of the Word of God.

2. 1 Peter 3:1-6

   a) Verse 1—"In the same manner, ye wives, be in subjection to your own husbands." The word *subjection*
   is the Greek word *hupotassō*. You may remember that
   it means "to come under the rank" and is a word of
   function, not essence. It's simply talking about the
   function of leadership and authority in the home. Peter also emphasizes the possessiveness that mitigates
   the submissive role ("your own husbands"). In other
   words, because the husband is the wife's possession,
   there is a natural sense of responding. Further, verse
   1 says, "If any [husbands] obey not the word, they
   also may without the word be won by the behavior of
   the wives."

   I'm glad Peter said this, because inevitably someone
   will say, "You don't know my husband. If I submit to
   him it's going to be awful. He's not a Christian, and
   he doesn't obey God or His Word. How in the world
   am I going to submit to this man?" That verse was
   written to answer that kind of response. Even if the
   husband doesn't obey the Word, the wife is to submit. And by her life the husband may be won. Wives,
   instead of writing "Repent" on the bottom of his beer
   cans, or pasting little notes in his lunch pail, or giving
   him another gospel presentation, set your life in response to God's ordained pattern for marriage. You
   may, without even using the Word of God, win him
   by your behavior.

   b) Verse 2—You may ask, "What kind of behavior will
   win my husband?" Peter answers, "Chaste conduct
   coupled with fear [reverence]." Wives should revere
   their husbands, manifesting a certain awe and respect. In other words, not only is her life chaste (pure
   behavior, conduct, and living), but there is also a reverence or an awe that looks up to him and respects
   him.

   c) Verse 3—If a wife is concerned with her husband—if
   she is in awe of him and if her conduct is chaste—her
   husband will not only be won by her attitude but also
   by its manifestation. Peter says in verse 3 that her

26

adorning will not be the "outward adorning of plaiting the hair [the weaving of gold and silver bands], and of wearing of gold or of putting on of apparel." In other words, if she preoccupies herself with such external adornment, she is in violation of the standard. Why? Because someone who is submissive doesn't call attention to herself.

d) Verse 4—Instead of being preoccupied with external adornment, verse 4 says, the woman should be concerned with "the hidden man of the heart," or "the secret of the heart" (the word *man* isn't in the Greek text). In other words, don't work on the outside; work on the inside. Instead of focusing on that which is corruptible (apparel, gold, braided hair), concentrate on developing "a meek and quiet spirit." The word *meek* (Gk., *praus*) means "quiet and gentle." The word *quiet* simply means "silent and still."

There are women today who are boisterous and loud, demanding their rights, parading and marching, and proclaiming the injustices done to them. That isn't God's standard. The Bible tells women instead to cultivate a meek, quiet, gentle, still, peaceful, silent spirit. Now that doesn't mean wives are to never offer their opinion. It means they are to understand that God expects them to be humble and still. That is the beauty and strength of a woman.

Note that all this is "in the sight of God." The Greek word *enōpion* means "face-to-face with." As you're standing face-to-face with God, He doesn't care what your hair looks like or how much gold you're wearing or if you have on the latest fashion; He's looking for a meek and quiet spirit. In His sight, a meek and quiet spirit is "of great price" (Gk., *poluteles*). *Poluteles* is the same word used in Mark 14:3, when the woman opened the alabaster box and took out the precious ointment. A meek and quiet spirit is precious and valuable to God.

e) Verse 5—"For after this manner in the old time the holy women also, who trusted in God, adorned themselves, being in subjection unto their own hus-

27

bands." That has always been the standard. Holy women focused on the inside. Why? Because they trusted God. They adorned themselves with a meek and quiet spirit in submission to their husbands.

f) Verse 6—Peter gives an illustration of one such woman: "Even as Sarah obeyed Abraham, calling him lord [a term of respect, awe, and reverence]; whose daughters ye are, as long as ye do well, and are not afraid with any terror." As Abraham is the father of the faithful (Gal. 3:7), Sarah is the mother of the submissive. Daughters of Sarah are those who call their husbands lord, are submissive to him, and "are not afraid with any terror."

I hear women say, "I'm afraid to submit to my husband, because if I do, I'll lose my rights. He'll run me down." But those holy women mentioned in 1 Peter 3:5 trusted God and had no fear of obeying Him. They knew that if there ever was an abuse, God would take care of the results. If you obey God and submit to your husband with a meek and quiet spirit, respond the way God wants you to respond, and don't have any fear in doing that, you can believe that God will honor your commitment—no matter what.

3. 1 Corinthians 11:3-12

There was a women's liberation movement in Corinth. Women were trying to do the same jobs as men and were trying to look and act like men. Apparently some of the women in the Corinthian church were swept up in that movement, and it was bringing reproach to the name of Christ and His church. So Paul wrote them to straighten it out.

In Corinthian society the women were supposed to be submissive; and the symbol of their submissiveness, modesty, and humility was that they wore a veil. Only two kinds of women took off their veils: prostitutes and feminists. The prostitutes took them off so men could see what they looked like, and the feminists took their veils off as a symbol of protest. So amid the feminists

28

and the harlots Paul writes to the Corinthian women and in effect says, "Ladies, keep your veils on. In our society that's recognized as submission. Respond to that symbol, so that the world doesn't see the church rebelling against a God-ordained principle." Paul is simply saying that a woman is to take a place of submission and that she should never violate that place.

4. Titus 2:3-5

Paul writes, "The aged women [the older, mature women whose children are no longer in the home] likewise, that they be in behavior as becometh holiness, not false accusers [they aren't scandalmongers, going around telling tales about people], not given to much wine, teachers of good things." Notice that the older women are to be teachers. And whom are they to teach? Verse 4 says, "That they may teach the young women." There is a remarkable pattern here. The older women are to teach the younger. Teach them what? "To be sober minded [to know their priorities], to love their husbands [Gk., *philandros*, "man-lover" or "husband-lover"]." Wives are to be characterized by their love for their husbands.

Some people emphasize that husbands are commanded to love their wives (Eph. 5:25) and that the wife is only a responder. They say to the husband, "If your wife doesn't love you or isn't responding properly to you, it's your fault; you're not loving her. All you need to do is love her, and she will respond." However, that's an overstatement because in Titus 2:4 wives are told to love their husbands. Again we see a tremendous mutuality and balance. The wife also has the responsibility to love her husband. Marriage is mutual.

Further, verse 4 says that mothers are to "love their children [Gk., *philateknos*, "child-lover"]." Remember, love involves self-sacrifice. Wives are to do whatever has to be done to meet the needs of their husbands and children. In fact, the implication of those terms is that the wife would even give her life for them.

Verse 5 says the older women are to teach the younger women "to be discreet, chaste, keepers at home, good, obedient to their own husbands, that the word of God be not blasphemed." The issue is that God wants His Word to be glorified, and when we don't live by His Word, it is dishonored. We are in effect saying, "Who cares what the Bible says?" So, if wives are to honor God's Word, they must love their husbands and children. Notice that the possession idea is again used with the phrase "their own husbands." Also notice the word *obedient*. That is a poor translation. The Greek word used here is not *hupakouō*, which means "to answer" or "to obey"; it is *hupotassō*, which means "to submit" or "to line up under." So again we see that women are to submit to their own husbands.

Should Mothers Be Employed Outside the Home?

We have a problem in America. There are more than 42 million working mothers in America, and 6 million of those have small children. One out of every three mothers with a child under three works in a full-time job. Who is to rear the children and take care of the home? I think the answer to this problem is contained in the phrase "keepers at home" in Titus 2:5.

The phrase "keepers at home" is the Greek word *oikourgos*. It comes from *oikos*, which means "home," and *ergon*, which means "work." *Oikourgos*, then, simply means "to work at home." I believe that means mothers ought to work at home. You may say, "But I have a wonderful job," "But we need the money," "But my kids are in school." However, the Bible says mothers are to work at home. It doesn't say, "Under some circumstances, this is not valid."

Now what does the word *ergon* mean? It refers to work, but the emphasis in the New Testament is that it involves a job or a task, and in some cases it is translated "employment." It is not referring to the quality of work; it is referring to an assigned task. A mother is to be employed in the assigned task of working at home. This use of *ergon* as an appointed employment, task, duty, or work is seen in the following passages: Mark 13:34, John 4:34, 17:4, Acts 13:2, Philippians 2:30, and 1 Thessalonians 5:13. Also, compare 1 Timothy 5:14, which says, "I will, therefore, that the younger women marry, bear children, guide the house." The phrase "guide the house" in the Greek text is *oikodespoteō*, and according to two excellent Greek lexicons (Arndt and Gingrich, Moulton and Milligan) that word means "to keep house."

So what's a mother to do with her life? Pursue a career? I don't see that here. According to Titus 2:3-5, a mother is to be a lover of her husband, a lover of her children, and one who does her task at home. A mother is to work inside the home—not outside.

I believe all this is related to the principle of being submissive to the husband. If a woman is working outside the home, she has a different set of circumstances to deal with: other involvements, other complications, other bosses, other people giving orders. The boss might say, "That's not the way to dress. I want you to dress this way." She may have to buy a new wardrobe, and if her husband doesn't agree with her boss's decision—there's conflict. I think a woman who works outside the home puts herself under circumstances and authorities that know no biblical injunction to be responsible for her.

Some of the problems we're seeing in our society today are directly related to the loss of mothers in the home. Now the issue is not whether the children are home from school yet. A mother's obligation to her home doesn't change just because her children are in school. In fact, psychological tests have shown that children who grow up in homes where the mother works are much more insecure than children who grow up in homes where the mother is home. When a child is in school, if he knows his mother is at home, that serves as an anchor.

The recent epidemic of working mothers has helped contribute to missing children, delinquency, adultery, fornication, divorce, and a lack of understanding about God-ordained roles in the home, to the detriment of the next generation. And by the way, mothers who stay home and do nothing but watch soap operas and behave like unfaithful busybodies are no better. Just because a mother stays home doesn't mean she's spiritual. Her influence might be worse than that of another mother who works.

Is a Wife to Be the Breadwinner of Her Family?

I tried to find a place in the Bible that says a wife may be the breadwinner. I didn't find it. I couldn't find any statement anywhere in the Bible that says the wife is to be the protector, the preserver, or the provider of the family. In fact, what I did find was just the opposite. First Timothy 5:8 talks about the husband's role and says, "If any provide not for his own, and specially for those of his own house, he hath denied the faith, and is worse than an infidel." The context here is that the man is to provide for any widow in his own house or immediate family, but it also extends to those in his extended family. The point is that the husband is to be the provider —not the wife.

What about the woman with children at home whose husband dies or divorces her, and she has to go to work? But if she leaves the home, the situation becomes even worse, because then no one would be at home. The father is not there, and now even the mother is gone. Who's responsible? If I'm related to such a person, I'm responsible to take up her support so that she can stay home. And if she doesn't have anyone related to her who can do that, the church is responsible. But she should not have to go out and forfeit the responsibility that God has given her.

And what are the older women whose children are all grown and out of the house to do? The answer is in Titus 2:3-5. When they were young women, they were to be loving their husbands and children and keeping their homes. Now that their children are grown, their priority should be to invest themselves in a spiritual ministry of teaching younger women. I'm not saying that at this point a woman can't work, but I don't see a provision for doing so in Scripture. She may take that liberty. However, I do know Scripture says that the responsibility of the older women is to teach the younger women. Think about it: if the younger women aren't staying at home and learning from the older women, the next generation won't have any older women who have anything to teach. There will be no legacy to pass on.

Now I know that some of you don't have a choice. No one is taking care of you or making provision for you. Some wives are working because no other family member is willing or able to work. But that is something the church is responsible for and has unfortunately neglected for centuries. The wife is not to be the breadwinner.

The Blessing of God or Disobedient Presumption?

In our society, when couples get married they may want a particular house or car and decide that in order to get it they will both have to work. Then, after they become accustomed to a life-style that demands two incomes, a child is born, the mother stays home for three months, the child is put in the lap of a baby-sitter, the mother goes back to work, and the baby-sitter raises the child. Even some Christian schools now provide day-care centers to take care of the children of the faculty and staff. But we cannot approach life that way and then say, "Look how the Lord has blessed us." If the husband is the provider and God gives the family twenty-five cars, a Greyhound bus, five houses, and a hotel—that's one thing. But if the mother has to violate the standard that God has ordained and leave the children to go to work to buy more material goods, don't confuse the blessing of God with disobedient presumption.

Working Mothers: A Contributing Factor to Inflation

Working mothers help contribute to inflation. When there are two breadwinners in the family, more earning power is created. More earning power creates higher prices, and higher prices create inflation. You may say, "But it's almost impossible to buy a house without two incomes." You might also note when the inflation spiral began—when mothers started going to work. But that is just a side issue, a matter for economists to debate. What's important is that Bible says mothers are to be "keepers at home."

Now you may say, "This is pretty strong stuff. I have a lot of energy and creativity, and I want to do things." Good. I have one more passage that I want you to look at.

5. Proverbs 31:10-31

If you think a mother is stifled in her God-ordained role, you've totally missed the point. Let's look at the virtuous woman of Proverbs 31.

a) Her value (v. 10)

"Her price is far above rubies [or pearls]."

b) Her trustworthiness (v. 11)

"The heart of her husband doth safely trust in her, so that he shall have no need of spoil." The first thing about a virtuous wife is that her husband can trust her with the checkbook without fearing that she's going to waste his fortune or squander his resources.

c) Her supportiveness (v. 12)

"She does him good, and not evil, all the days of her life." She sees herself as one who supports her husband and undergirds him, freeing him from anxiety and fear. And she doesn't just sit around saying supportive things; she gets into the action.

d) Her productiveness (vv. 13-14)

She seeks wool and flax, and if she has to travel as a merchant's ship to get the best deal, she does it. Now I've never said that a woman has to stay at home and never leave. She may have a ministry, disciple people, attend a Bible study, or shop. Obviously, there are places she has to go if she's going to be productive. The woman of Proverbs 31 goes a long way to get a good deal on wool and flax, and according to verse 19, when she gets it she puts it on the spindle and the distaff and makes thread. And with that thread she begins to make clothes. She's productive.

e) Her sacrifice (v. 15)

"She riseth also while it is yet night, and giveth food to her household, and a portion to her maidens." She's more concerned about her family than her own comfort. Her primary concern is to serve her family.

f) Her enterprise (vv. 16-19)

She saves up money and instead of squandering it buys a field, purchases some seed, and plants a vineyard. There's a place for enterprise, but the home must be the base. The wife's earnings should not be the source of the family's income. If a family can't live on what the husband makes, then they're living beyond their God-intended means and victimized by our affluent, materialistic, indulgent society. And if God prospers a family through the husband, thank Him, praise Him, and enjoy it—because God gives bountifully.

In verse 17 we see that the virtuous woman is not frail and self-indulgent, making herself beautiful all the time. She works with her arms to provide a little extra—not because her family needs it for the moment or because she's being indulgent, but because she's planning for the future against the moment when tragedy might come (the Hebrew text in verse 25 says she'll laugh at the future).

g) Her priorities (vv. 20-24)

I want to show you why she is so enterprising. There's a progression here.

(1) Verse 20—She's enterprising, first of all, so that she can give to those who don't have anything.

(2) Verse 21—Since she had something left over from what she gave to the needy, she clothed her household in scarlet so they would have something a little nicer.

(3) Verse 22—After the needs of the needy were met and the family had nice clothing, she made herself something nice—a lined overcoat out of tapestry and clothes of white linen and purple.

(4) Verse 24—After she met the needs of the poor, the needs of her family, and her own needs, she started a little business out of the home, making

35

fine linen, selling it, and delivering belts to the merchant. And notice that it is all in the right sequence of priority.

    h) Her reward (vv. 27-28)

"She looketh well to the ways of her household, and eateth not the bread of idleness. Her children rise up and call her blessed; her husband, also, and he praiseth her." That's the prize for living out God's perfect design.

B. The Manner of Submission (v. 22*b*)

"As unto the Lord."

Wives, when you submit to your husbands, it shouldn't be with the attitude, "I'll do it, but this is really rough. If you only knew what I was sacrificing for the sake of spirituality." You are to submit "as unto the Lord." If Jesus Christ walked up to you and said, "Woman, quit your job and go home and take care of your children," what would you say? What if your husband walked up to you and said that? The Lord has appointed your husband as head of your marriage and family. Obey him as you would the Lord.

C. The Motive of Submission (v. 23*a*)

"For the husband is the head of the wife."

Wives, you are the body, and your husband is the head. The head gives the orders; the body doesn't. You may say, "But that is degrading." No it isn't. When a body responds to its head, it isn't degraded; but when a body doesn't respond to the head, it's considered spastic. When we see a body responding to the mind, a well-coordinated functioning body, the body is honored as well as the mind. But if the body doesn't respond, both are dishonored.

D. The Model of Submission (vv. 23*b*-24)

"Even as Christ is the head of the church; and he is the savior of the body. Therefore, as the church is subject unto

Christ, so let the wives be to their own husbands in everything."

Jesus Christ is the Savior of the church, and when He died on the cross He said, "It is finished" (John 19:30). All we need to do is fall under His provision. That's the illustration. Now in the home, the husband is the provider, the deliverer, the protector, and the savior. We don't need co-breadwinners, co-saviors, co-protectors, co-providers, or co-preservers. All a wife needs to do is fall under the protection, the provision, and the preservation of her husband. That's God's ordained pattern. And believe me, when we follow that pattern, we'll have happier homes, godlier children, and fewer divorces. God will be honored, and the Word of God will not be blasphemed.

Finally, verse 24 says that the wives are to submit in everything. You may ask, "In *everything?*" Yes. There is only one exception. If your husband tells you to do something that is disobedient to God, then you must say what Peter said: "We ought to obey God rather than men" (Acts 5:29). But short of that, everything. What's the key? Being "filled with the Spirit" (v. 18). The Spirit-filled wife will submit to her husband, and God's Word will be honored as a result.

Focusing on the Facts

1. Explain the difference between the Greek word used to describe the submission of the wife in Ephesians 5:22 and the word used to describe the submission of children and slaves in Ephesians 6:1, 5 (see pp. 23-24).
2. Is Paul's command to wives an implication that they are inferior? Explain (see p. 24).
3. Why is the wife to be subject to the leadership of her husband (see p. 24)?
4. What has been the foundation of laws in societies influenced by God (see p. 25)?
5. Why is the issue of authority and submission in the home not popular (see p. 25)?
6. How can a non-believing husband be won to Christ by his believing wife (1 Pet. 3:1; see p. 26)?

7. Instead of being preoccupied with external adornment, what does 1 Peter 3:4 say that a woman should be concerned with? What kind of spirit should she develop? Why (see p. 27)?

8. What was the symbol of submissiveness in Corinthian society? What kinds of women did not identify themselves with that symbol? Why did Paul want them to use it (see pp. 28-29)?

9. Whom are older Christian women supposed to teach? What are they supposed to teach (see p. 29)?

10. Is a wife only a responder to her husband's love? Explain (see p. 29).

11. Where is a mother to work according to Titus 2:5 (see p. 30)?

12. How can a wife's submissiveness be challenged if she works outside the home (see p. 31)?

13. How can a child benefit from knowing that his mother is at home (see p. 31)?

14. According to 1 Timothy 5:8, who is to be the breadwinner of the family (see p. 32)?

15. If a mother is divorced or widowed, should she have to work to support herself and her children? Where should her support come from if possible (see p. 32)?

16. What often happens when young married couples who have become accustomed to a two-income life-style decide to have children (see p. 33)?

17. Does a mother's energy and creativity become stifled in her God-ordained role? Describe the woman of Proverbs 31 (see pp. 33-36).

18. What progression of priorities can be seen in the enterprising efforts of the virtuous woman in Proverbs 31 (see pp. 35-36)?

19. Describe the manner of submission that should characterize a wife (see p. 36).

20. Explain how the model of the church's submission to Christ applies to the submission of the wife to her husband (see pp. 36-37).

21. What is the one time when a wife need not submit to her husband (Acts 5:29)? What is the key to submitting "in everything" (Eph. 5:18, 24; see p. 37)?

Pondering the Principles

1. Read 1 Peter 3:1-6. As evidence of a wife's submission to her husband, what type of conduct should she have? What type of attitude should she develop? What effect can submissiveness

have on an unbelieving husband? If you are a wife, rate your submissiveness to your husband: (1) always, in everything; (2) usually, except when I don't fully agree with him; (3) sometimes, when the issue is insignificant or I'm too tired to argue; or (4) seldom, because he isn't a Christian. Do you submit to him as you would "unto the Lord" (Eph. 5:22)? You are bringing honor to yourself and your husband when you willingly submit to his leadership. Even if your husband doesn't know the Lord, the beauty of your submissive spirit, which is empowered by the Holy Spirit who indwells you, can draw him to the point of submission to God. If he knows you are his best friend and are always ready to support him rather than to criticize him, he may be willing to follow the God your reverent life reflects.

2. If you are a mother who works outside the home, analyze why you are working. By the time taxes, increased child-care, clothing, and transportation expenses are deducted from your income, how much extra income are you actually providing? Does an exhausting day at work determine the way you handle discipline problems in the evening, as well as the quality of attention you give your children? If you are separated or divorced and have the power to reverse that situation, try to do so. As a single parent, you will be faced with the dilemma of having someone else raise your children or having no provision for your children as you raise them. Trust God to provide for your needs through a husband (1 Tim. 5:14), a family member (1 Tim. 5:4, 8), a government subsidy, or an adequate amount of life insurance to replace the potential loss of your husband's income so that you can fulfill the biblical role of a mother.

3
The Divine Pattern for Marriage—Part 3
The Wife's Priorities

Outline

Introduction

Review
I. The Duty of the Wife (vv. 22-24)
   A. The Matter of Submission (v. 22*a*)
      1. Colossians 3:18
      2. 1 Peter 3:1-6
      3. 1 Corinthians 11:3-12
      4. Titus 2:3-5
      5. Proverbs 31:10-31

Lesson
      6. 1 Timothy 5:3-16
      7. Genesis 3:16
   B. The Manner of Submission (v. 22*b*)
   C. The Motive of Submission (v. 23*a*)
   D. The Model of Submission (v. 23*b*-24)

Introduction

The Christian standard of living is different from that of the world. As believers we are to be salt and light in a decaying and dark society. God calls us to be different. Unfortunately, that isn't easy when we become victims of society. Sometimes, we become so deeply engulfed in the world's system that even though God's Word speaks clearly on certain issues, we have a difficult time hearing, understanding, and applying its teaching.

Over and over, the New Testament calls us to another level of living, another style of life, another dimension of existence. It calls us to new thinking, new talking, new acting, and new ministries. For example we are to "set [our affections] on things above, not on things on the earth" (Col. 3:2); we are to "put on the new man" (Eph. 4:24; cf. Col. 3:10); we are to "walk worthy of the vocation to which [we] are called" (Eph. 4:1); and we no longer walk as the Gentiles walk or function as the world functions (Eph. 4:17). In other words, we have been translated from the "power of darkness" into the "kingdom of [God's] dear Son" (Col. 1:13).

We don't think as the world thinks; we don't act as the world acts; we don't talk as the world talks; we don't set goals that the world sets; and we don't do the things that the world does. We are called to be distinct. Our distinction is our identification with God. The hope of humanity is that in seeing the distinction they would be drawn to Jesus Christ. The whole objective for the believer is to be unique, different, set apart. And the key is in Ephesians 5:18: "Be filled with the Spirit." The only thing that will separate us from the world is to be filled with the Spirit of God. If we're filled with the things of the world, there will be no difference.

I realize that sometimes it is difficult to live by the Spirit. We are often too preoccupied with a system that has infiltrated our thinking and tried to push us into its mold. But as believers, we belong to Jesus Christ and are to think differently from the way the world thinks. That goal becomes specific when we start talking about marriage and the home.

Review

I. THE DUTY OF THE WIFE (vv. 22-24)

A. The Matter of Submission (v. 22a; see pp. 23-36)

1. Colossians 3:18 (see pp. 24-25)

2. 1 Peter 3:1-6 (see pp. 26-28)

3. 1 Corinthians 11:3-12 (see pp. 28-29)

4. Titus 2:3-5 (see pp. 29-30)

5. Proverbs 31:10-31 (see pp. 33-36)

The Jewish View of Wives' Duties

The Mishna is the codification of Jewish law. It gives standards of Jewish behavior and reveals the attitudes the Jews had at the time of Christ, some of which were inherited from their Old Testament roots. The Mishna has several things to say regarding the home and the duties of wives.

1. Household duties

   The wife was to grind flour, bake, launder, cook, nurse her children, make the beds, spin wool, prepare the children for school, and take the children to school to ensure their arrival.

2. Employment

   a) Alongside her husband

      From the Mishna, we know that some women did work together with their husbands in the fields picking fruit—but it was always alongside of and in support of their husbands.

      According to the Mishna, there were some women who worked apart from their husbands in the marketplace. They were considered to be a disgrace to society.

   b) In the home

      A wife could work at crafts or horticulture in the home and sell the fruits of her labor. That was sometimes done to supplement the husband's income or to be used as pocket money for personal use.

3. Adornment

   Although a housewife was kept busy with her work in the house, she was still expected to adorn herself properly. That point was stressed in many traditions.

4. Philanthropy

Apart from strictly household work, the wife was also responsible for hospitality and the care of guests. Wives were active in charitable work, giving alms to poor people who came to their houses and participating in charitable projects outside the home.

The Jewish laws were clear: the woman's priority was in the home. She was to take care of all the needs of her home, her children, her husband, strangers, the poor and needy, and guests. Then she could work alongside her husband to assist him in his work. And if she had any time left over, she could be as enterprising as she wanted (e.g. Prov. 31:10-31).

Understanding the Priorities

It's sad to think what the next generation of mothers is going to be like if they don't understand their priorities. The responsibility to rear children is in the home. Proverbs 1:8-9 says that a child is not only to listen to his father's instruction but also to the law of his mother. A wife is to take care of her husband's needs, to be supportive of his life and career, and to work alongside him, ministering to him. She is also to build up her own spiritual life so that she can be a godly mother to her children, always available in a crisis and there to teach them. Often those times of teaching and interaction take preparation, but that's a priority. Don't believe that God expects a mother to work full time so that she can send her children to a Christian school; the Christian school will never be able to overcome the lack of commitment on the part of the mother. If she is not preoccupied with spiritual instruction and committed to teaching her children the things of God, the school will never be able to override the impact of that testimony in the home.

When a wife has fulfilled all those priorities in the home, then she has a responsibility to help the needy and the poor and to be involved in ministering to people. Christian mothers in the home during the day could be a valuable resource to their neighborhood and community. When the priorities are met and a mother has time left over, she may want to pursue something that's enterprising and creative, and that's fine. But she needs to fulfill the priorities first.

Lesson

6. 1 Timothy 5:3-16

I want to illustrate the woman's role in the home and her priorities by looking at this passage on the care of widows.

a) Verse 3—"Honor widows that are widows indeed." Widows without resources ("widows indeed") are to be cared for and supported ("honor" means pay, cf. v. 17) and not forced to go to work, again reinforcing that a woman is to have her ministry in the home. I believe the principle of supporting a widow without resources could even be applied, for example, to a believing wife whose unbelieving husband commits adultery and forsakes her—leaving her with children at home. She should not be forced to go to work. A woman who has no resources is to be paid. Verse 4 tells us who should take care of her.

b) Verse 4—"If any widow have children or nephews, let them learn first to show piety at home, and to requite their parents; for that is good and acceptable before God." If a man is related to a widow without resources, he is to practice his Christianity in the home by supplying her need before practicing it in the church. Again, that is so she can stay in the home —where God wants her to be.

c) Verse 5—"Now she that is a widow indeed, and desolate, trusteth in God, and continueth in supplications and prayers night and day." What is a woman to do when she becomes a desolate widow? Is she to immediately check out the classified ads? No. She is to fall on her knees and beseech God for some source of supply. She is to cast herself upon God's mercy. That is why the Bible tells us to meet the needs of widows. James 1:27 says, "Pure religion and undefiled before God and the Father is this: to visit the fatherless and widows in their affliction." That is the responsibility of the people of God—and it always has been.

45

So the widow is to pray and seek God; however, the alternative is in verse 6.

d) Verse 6—"She that liveth in pleasure is dead while she liveth." The phrase "liveth in pleasure" is from the Greek word *spatalē*, which gives the idea of living in wanton luxury—pleasure madness. If she chooses to live that way, she is as dead as her husband. Why? Because she is deadening herself to God's standards. There are just two alternatives here. Either she is on her knees praying for God's supply or she's out living in the world. Notice this passage doesn't give working as an alternative; she is to be cared for.

e) Verse 7—"These things command, that they may be blameless." These principles are not optional or just something to think about; they are commands. To disobey is to be blamed.

f) Verse 8—"If any provide not for his own, and specially for those of his own house, he hath denied the faith, and is worse than an infidel [unbeliever]." That is serious. We talk about a lot of sins in the Bible, but you don't hear too many sermons on this verse. Men need to support the widows in need who are related to them. Rather than force widows to work for their own support, men are to care for them—that's God's standard. And if they don't, they are to be blamed because they are in reality denying the faith. Why? Because the Christian faith embodies providing for widows. Also, not supporting them would be worse than what unbelievers do, because many of them care for their widows.

You may ask, "What if there are no men around who can support a widow?" According to verse 16, if there is no man who can be the resource, then a believing woman may step in: "If any man or woman that believeth have widows, let them relieve them." (Note that the phrase "man or" in verse 16 is not in the most accurate manuscripts.) The believing women who have resources may minister to widows by providing them with lodging, daily meals, or clothing.

You may ask, "Who provides for the widow who doesn't have any relatives to care for her?" The end of verse 16 says, "And let not the church be charged, that it may relieve them that are widows indeed." If there is no man and no woman to do it, then the church should. And that doesn't necessarily mean the church will budget in such an expense. It means that the people who make up the community of faith can reach out to that widow in need.

The point of the passage is this: a woman is to be cared for and not left to her own resources—especially when there is no father or man in the home. She is to fall on the mercy of God, who then extends this directive first to the men, then to the women, and then to the church: "Gather that widow in your arms!" And that is precisely what the early church did (Acts 2:44-45; 4:32-35; 6:1-6).

g) Verse 9—"Let not a widow be taken into the number under sixty years old." The phrase "taken into the number" refers to the widow list of the early church. Two rules applied to the list: (1) the church would take on the full support of widows who reached the age of sixty; and (2) those who joined the list became part of the group of widows who represented the church in an official ministry.

There were prerequisites to being put on the list other than being sixty years old or more. The first one is at the end of verse 9: "Having been the wife of one man." In other words, a one-man woman, one who was absolutely devoted and loving to her husband. That does not necessarily rule out a divorce or having been married more than once; it refers to the intensity of her commitment to the man who was her husband. She was to be a woman who loved her husband.

h) Verse 10—A further prerequisite was that she be "well reported of for good works." She had to have a reputation for doing good. What were some of those good works? "If she hath brought up children." Notice that she didn't just bear them; she brought them up. Not only that but "if she hath lodged strangers." She had to be available for hospitality, having a home where there was always food, a warm place of receptivity, and a bed for someone who needed it. She also had to have "washed the saints' feet . . . relieved the afflicted . . . [and] diligently followed every good work."

i) Verses 11-16—Summing up these verses, Paul basically says, "Don't put the younger widows on the list." Why? Because it would be difficult for the young widows to keep their commitment as "official widows." They would begin their ministry in total devotion and service to Christ, but after a period of time many would notice men and desire to get married again. Once that happened, their ministry would no longer appeal to them, and they would put aside their commitment. Without a total commitment to Christ, the continued financial support of the church, instead of enabling them to maintain a godly life-style, would cause them to "learn to be idle, wandering about from house to house; and not only idle but tattlers also, and busybodies, speaking things which they ought not" (v. 13).

Therefore, the younger widows ought to "marry, bear children, rule [keep] the house, give no occasion to the adversary to speak reproachfully. For some have already turned aside after Satan" (vv. 14-15). A younger widow was not to be put on the church's widow list; she was to be remarried and get back in the home with a husband who would then take over her care. She was to bear children and be a keeper at home. And again, we're right back to that divine priority.

The Choice Is Yours

You have to choose the level at which you want to live. The Bible doesn't say women can't work. But you have to determine whether you're going to take the highest standard or something less. Psalm 113 implies that motherhood is God's highest calling for a woman.

Not all women are called to be married or have children, but still the choice is yours.

Hannah lived at the highest level of divine priority (1 Sam. 1:21-23). Her husband, Elkanah, asked her to go on a trip with him to the Temple before her little baby, Samuel, had been fully weaned (lit., "fully dealt with"). But Hannah wouldn't go. She wouldn't leave her child. And according to what we know from the apocryphal writings, the age of being "fully dealt with" was at least three years of age. Until she had fully dealt with that child in terms of physical feeding and the spiritual input he needed until he was three, she wouldn't take him on a trip because that would disrupt her time with him.

Is Your Moral Character Being Undermined?

Mothers, there is no sense in staying home if you are watching soap operas and polluting your mind. Few things will corrupt the mind as subtly as will watching television programs all day long. You cannot sit and watch garbage without its undermining your moral character. There's no virtue in being at home unless a spiritual purpose is being accomplished.

7. Genesis 3:16

Why is there so much rebellion against God-ordained priorities in marriage and the family? Genesis 1:27-28 says, "So God created man in his own image, in the image of God created he him; male and female created he them. And God blessed them, and God said unto them, Be fruitful and multiply; and fill the earth, and subdue it; and have dominion." Notice that even though God made woman to be a suitable helper (Gen. 2:18), and even though He made the man to be the head (1 Cor. 11:3-12; 1 Tim. 2:11-15), God said to them, "Be fruitful and multiply . . . fill the earth . . . subdue it; and have dominion." They were co-regents. They ruled together. The principles of leadership and submission aren't even visible because prior to sin the relationship was so beautiful, so God-ordained, and so pure that they multiplied together, filled the earth together, subdued the earth together, and ruled together. But in Genesis 3, sin enters into the picture, and immediately they are cursed.

a) "Unto the woman he said, I will greatly multiply thy sorrow and thy conception."

In other words, the pain of childbirth was to be a constant reminder to every woman who would ever live that she is a victim of sin. That is part of the curse, but there's more.

b) "And thy desire shall be to thy husband, and he shall rule over thee."

(1) What it does not mean

Most commentators say that this means that it's normal for a wife to have a strong sexual and psychological dependence on her husband, and that it's normal for her to desire the man and for the man to rule over her. But that can't be the interpretation.

(*a*) Sexually, in most cases, the man has a much stronger desire for physical fulfillment with a woman than a woman does for a man.

(*b*) Historically, women have never loved their role of submission to their husbands. There isn't a period in history where women weren't chafing underneath male authority.

(*c*) If this was just the normal desire, it wouldn't be a curse; before the Fall, the woman was wonderfully submissive and dependent on the man. So whatever the meaning of this passage is, it must be something different from what it was before the curse.

(2) What it does mean

    (a) "And he shall rule over thee"

The word translated "rule" is *masal* in Hebrew. It means "to reign" or "to rule." In the Septuagint (the Greek translation of the Old Testament) the word is *kathistēmi*, which means "to install in an office" or "to elevate to an official position." So, as part of the curse, God in effect said to the woman, "You were once co-regents, wonderfully ruling together as a team, but from now on the man is installed over you." That was a new kind of ruling—an authority that had never been known before. Regarding the word *masal*, C. F. Keil states: "Created for the man, the woman was made subordinate to him from the very first; but the supremacy of the man was not intended to become a despotic rule" (*Biblical Commentary on the Old Testament*, vol. 1 [Grand Rapids: Eerdmans, 1971], p. 103). But in the Fall, that's what it became. Eve usurped the leadership of Adam when she took the fruit. The curse on the woman is that man is going to rule over her. But that's only half the picture.

    (b) "And thy desire shall be to thy husband"

The word *desire* is the Hebrew word *tshuka*. This word is used only one other time in the Pentateuch, fifteen verses later in 4:7. *Tshuka* comes from an Arabic root that means "to compel, to impel, to urge, to seek control." Notice it does not come from the Arabic root for "exciting," "loving," or "psychological desire." To get a feeling for what Genesis 3:16 is saying, look at how *tshuka* is translated in 4:7. The best textual rendering of this verse is: "Sin will desire to master you [or control you], but you must master it." In other words, God said to Cain, "Now Cain, sin will desire to control you, but you must master

51

it." The word *desire* in Genesis 4:7 (*tshuka*) is the same word, in the same grammatical structure, in an absolutely identical form as the word in 3:16. So, whatever the word means in 4:7, it will also mean back in 3:16 because it's in the same context. Therefore, 3:16 would read: "Your desire will be to control your husband, but he will rule over you."

The woman usurped the place of the man, and she was cursed: "He shall rule over thee." In other words, the man would subdue her tendency to control him. And because Adam followed the lead of Eve (3:17), God added to this curse and said, in effect, "From now on she's going to keep seeking to control you."

Is There an Answer to the Curse?

As part of the curse of God on the sin of Adam and Eve, God essentially said, "Family life is going to be impossible without Me. In the same way that you are going to have to fight the weeds in the ground to grow food, you are going to have a fight in your marriage. In marriage, the woman's desire will be to control the man, and he will have to subdue her." That's why we have women pushing for equal rights and male chauvinists crushing them down. So what's the answer? The curse is erased in Jesus Christ. When people know and love the Lord Jesus Christ and are filled with the Spirit, wives will submit to their husbands; and husbands, instead of being dictators, will love their wives as Christ loved the church. When that takes place, we're right back to the way it was before the Fall.

Women have been oppressed by the crushing power of men who want to keep them subdued; men have been hassled by women who want to rise to the top and take over—but Christians have the answer: Jesus Christ. When Christ comes into people's lives and the Spirit of God fills them, men and women submit to the God-ordained pattern, and the home becomes as it was in the Garden before the Fall. Together they're fruitful, together they multiply, together they have dominion, together they subdue, and together they work out the plan of God in their lives. Christianity is not offering to the world the suppression of women and the exaltation of men (or vice versa). Christianity offers, through Jesus Christ and the power of the Holy Spirit, the perfection of men and women in their God-ordained and God-created roles. And when that happens, and the home becomes the place where spiritual life functions, God will raise up a godly seed and perpetuate it into the next generation.

B. The Manner of Submission (v. 22b; see p. 36)

C. The Motive of Submission (v. 23a; see p. 36)

D. The Model of Submission (v. 23b-24; see pp. 36-37)

Focusing on the Facts

1. How are Christians expected to live in a morally decaying and spiritually dark society? Why is it hard to live like that (see pp. 41-42)?
2. Why are Christians not to do the things the world does? What is the key to being able to separate oneself from the world (see p. 42)?
3. Where was the woman's priority according to Jewish law contained in the Mishna (see pp. 43-44)?
4. What priorities does a Christian mother have with regard to her family? What should her secondary priorities be (see p. 44)?
5. How are widows without resources to be honored according to 1 Timothy 5:3-4, 8? Through whom has God designed for her needs to be met (see pp. 45-46)?
6. What did the early church do for widows who had no other resources and who had reached the age of sixty (see p. 47)?
7. Identify some of the prerequisites that had to be met to put a widow on the church's list. Where do they imply that she spent most of her time (see pp. 47-48)?
8. What were younger widows obligated to do (see p. 48)?
9. What element of the curse would be a reminder to women that they are victims of sin (Gen. 3:16; see p. 50)?

10. What type of desire would the wife have for her husband when evaluated in light of Genesis 4:7, where the same Hebrew word is used? How was that a curse upon Adam (see pp. 51-52)?
11. How can the conflict of women's liberation and male chauvinism resolved? Explain (see p. 52).
12. What will happen to the home when men and women are perfected in their God-ordained roles? What will God raise up as a result of that (see p. 53)?

Pondering the Principles

1. Is your home a place that highlights your uniqueness in Christ? Do the relationships among your family members reflect lives that are focused on godly values and directed by the Spirit? When people walk into your home, do they sense an orderliness and a peacefulness that should characterize every Christian home? Meditate as a family on Colossians 3:12-21, using those verses as a guideline for a devotional time together. Determine what qualities mentioned in the passage are lacking or weak in your family. Confess to one another the wrong attitudes and actions each has been exhibiting. After you choose an area you need to concentrate on, pray for one another that each may be strengthened to live the quality of life that glorifies Christ.

2. Does your church have a ministry to widows? Is it taking the responsibility to care for godly widows who have no other means of support? If not, would you be instrumental in praying with your pastor about such a ministry and helping to initiate it? As a preventative measure against the church's being overburdened (1 Tim. 5:16), consider having a financial planner or tax adviser give a seminar to your church members on how they can prepare for the premature death of a breadwinner and their retirement years. They might also suggest some effective ways that dependent widows can be assisted through trusts providing the donor with tax advantages.

3. If you are a mother who is staying at home with your children, are you taking advantage of your opportunity to shape their lives for godly living? Or is your time spent unproductively with television programs that might be tearing down the very

principles you are trying to instill into your life and your children's? Make sure every day has spiritual input so that your children begin looking at life from God's perspective. Prepare them for society's secular influence by teaching godly values (Prov. 22:6; 2 Tim. 3:15).

4
The Divine Pattern for Marriage—Part 4
The Role of the Husband

Outline

Introduction
A. The Curse of God
  1. Marriage before the curse (Gen. 2:18-25; cf. 1:27-28)
    a) Authority and submission
    b) Unity
  2. Marriage after the curse (Gen. 3:16)
    a) The elements of the curse
      (1) Pain in childbearing (3:16*a*)
      (2) Strife in marriage (3:16*b*)
      (3) Work (3:17-19)
      (4) Death (2:17)
    b) The effects of the curse
B. The Corruption of Satan
C. The Confusion of Society

Review
  I. The Duty of the Wife (vv. 22-24)

Lesson
 II. The Duty of the Husband (vv. 25-33)
    A. The Manner of Love (vv. 25-31)

Introduction

Field-Marshal Montgomery once said to his young troops, "Gentlemen, don't even think of marriage until you have mastered the art of warfare." Why is marriage potential warfare? Why is it so difficult to have a meaningful relationship with someone? The most meaningful relationship is that which occurs between a man and a woman in a marriage, yet fulfillment is elusive. Having a meaningful, lasting relationship that gets better, richer, and more fulfilling is rare. In fact, whenever we see marriage portrayed, it's usually depicted as a discontented, bitter relationship ending in separation or divorce. There are reasons for that.

A. The Curse of God

1. Marriage before the curse (Gen. 2:18-25; cf. 1:27-28)

a) Authority and submission

In Genesis 2 God says, "It is not good that the man should be alone; I will make him an help fit for him [or "suitable helper"]. . . . And Adam gave names to all cattle, and to the fowl of the air, and to every beast of the field; but for Adam there was not found an help fit for him" (vv. 18, 20). And in verses 21-22 God provides a suitable helper to aid Adam as he rules the pure and undefiled world of creation. Notice that from the beginning, God designed someone to be in charge and someone to help; someone to be in authority and someone to be submissive; someone to be the leader and someone to be the follower; someone to take care of the provisions and someone to be provided for. The man had the role of leadership, and the woman had the role of the follower. The man protected, provided, preserved, and cared for the woman. She was a fitting, or suitable, helper for him.

b) Unity

Adam meets his wife in verse 23 and says, "This is now bone of my bones, and flesh of my flesh; she shall be called Woman, because she was taken out of Man." The chapter continues, "Therefore shall a man leave his father and his mother, and shall cleave unto his wife; and they shall be one flesh. And they were both naked, the man and his wife, and were not ashamed" (vv. 24-25). Here was a perfect relationship. Adam saw Eve as one with him in every sense —that was God's design. He was the leader, and she was to follow his lead; he had responsibility for her, and she was under his responsibility. The woman's submissiveness was willing, and the man's provision was willing. There was no animosity—no struggle or fighting—nothing but a perfectly glorious union. That union is also illustrated in a brief account in 1:27-28, where they are described as being fruitful and multiplying, filling the earth, subduing it, and having dominion together as co-regents. That doesn't deny the authority and submission principle; it just shows that they existed in oneness.

Four Reasons for Marriage

1. To propagate children (Gen. 1:28)

2. To eliminate solitude (Gen. 2:18)

3. To prevent immorality (1 Cor. 7:2)

4. To provide enjoyment (Heb. 13:4; Gen. 26:8)

2. Marriage after the curse (Gen. 3:16)

God made marriage a beautiful relationship: the woman was to be the helper, supporting the man, and the man was to be the head, loving the woman. The woman's submission was willing, the man's love dominated his actions, and their union was beautiful—but something terrible happened in Genesis 3.

The serpent, bypassing the leadership of the man, went straight to the woman, who was by nature the follower (because he knew she would give him a better audience), and enticed her to do the one thing God told her not to do: eat from the tree of the knowledge of good and evil. She took the fruit, ate it, and gave it to her husband. Here we see a role reversal. The woman usurped the leadership of the man, and he became the follower. God's design for marriage was twisted—and marriage has been defiled ever since. If you want to know why marriage is tough, it's because there has been, since that act, a role reversal.

In Genesis 3:16-19 God gives a curse to the man and woman because of their sin. We find that the most basic elements of human life are involved.

a) The elements of the curse

(1) Pain in childbearing (3:16*a*)

The wonderful reality and the glorious anticipation, joy, and hope of having a child would be somewhat overshadowed by the anguish of childbirth.

(2) Strife in marriage (3:16*b*)

There would be a problem in marriage caused by the man's ruling over the woman oppressively and the woman's seeking to rule over the man (see pp. 49-53).

(3) Work (3:17-19)

Man would need to work to earn a living and provide for his family.

(4) Death (2:17)

God had said to Adam, "For in the day that thou eatest thereof thou shalt surely die."

Pain in childbirth, problems in the home, difficulty in getting food, and death are all a result of the sin in the Garden. When Adam sinned, his death and his sin "passed upon all men" (Rom. 5:12). The human race was cursed.

Few in our society will deny there is pain in childbirth or that it is difficult for a man to earn a living and provide for his family. But people don't want to admit that one reason there is conflict in marriage is the reversal of roles that started with the original sin.

b) The effects of the curse

If you want to know why we have women's liberation movements, it's partly because the element of the curse that says women will seek to rule over men is still in effect. Male oppression and male chauvinism are evident because that part of the curse is also in effect. Women's liberation and male chauvinism are simply manifestations of depravity, the Fall of man, and the curse.

How to Have a Marriage That Works

Two things are needed if you're going to have a marriage that works.

1. A woman characterized by submission

A woman must go back to that place of beautiful submission she knew before the Fall.

2. A man characterized by sacrificial love

A man must go back to the place where his commitment is to love the woman and do for her everything he would do for himself—as he did before the Fall.

Do you want to know why we have problems in marriage? Because marriage is cursed to begin with. Depravity manifests itself in two sinful people—in the woman as she seeks to overrule the man, and in the man as he crushes the woman. Husbands who love their wives don't do so because it's the natural thing to do. It's natural to love ourselves—to be self-consumed and self-absorbed. And as long as a man is like that, he can't give himself in love to someone else.

61

Men fulfill their part of the curse too. Women have been abused. Men in our society aren't any different from those of the past: they suppress women, crush them down, and make them into sex objects. As a result, we have a proliferation of pornography, and magazines, movies, and advertising often portray women as creatures with no function other than that of fulfilling the sexual desires of men. That perspective is wrong—it makes woman into something far less than God ever intended her to be.

Men have oppressed women, and women have sought to override the bounds of their God-given design. We can't expect anything different because that's the legacy of sin. However, it doesn't have to be that way. It possible to have a marriage relationship where the wife is lifted up, exalted, and allowed to be all that God intended her to be and where the husband knows how to invest his life in lovingly providing for her. Such a co-regency fulfills the plan that God intended.

B. The Corruption of Satan

It's bad enough that marriage is cursed, but that isn't all: Satan tries to destroy marriages also. If we add Satan's influence to the initial curse, we're going to have major problems. In Genesis, we find that as soon as sin entered the world, Satan began to attack marriage. He tried to dissolve and crush marriage as best he could because he knew it was the only hope of right human relationships. He wanted to devastate the world by destroying relationships at their most important level—in the home. So immediately after the Fall in Genesis 3, Satan tries to corrupt marriage in the following ways.

1. Polygamy (Gen. 4:19, 23)

2. Evil sexual thoughts and words (Gen. 9:22)

3. Adultery (Gen. 16:1-3)

4. Homosexuality (Gen. 19:4-11)

5. Fornication and rape (Gen. 34:1-2)

6. Incest (Gen. 38:13-18)

7. Prostitution (Gen. 38:24)

8. Seduction (Gen. 39:7-12)

Do you want to know why marriage is tough? Do you want to know why there are so many divorces, so many miserable people, and so many unhappy relationships? It all started when the woman took the place of man and acted independently. When the man fell submissively to the woman in sin, God locked marriage in chains. And since that time, women by nature desire to rule men, and men tend to despotically dominate women. Add to that the impulses of polygamy, evil thoughts and words, adultery, homosexuality, fornication, rape, unequally yoked relationships (Gen. 34), incest, prostitution, and seduction, and you'll have trouble trying to have a successful marriage.

C. The Confusion of Society

If the elements of the curse and the corruptions of Satan aren't enough to make marriage difficult, add to them a society that extols all of Satan's corruptions as virtuous. It's tough living a godly life in this evil and perverse generation. The only people who can are those who: (1) know the Lord Jesus Christ (Eph. 1-3) and (2) are filled with His Spirit (Eph. 5:18). Apart from that, a person has no more hope of making a marriage work the way God designed it than of finding a pot of gold at the end of a rainbow. It will never happen.

At the heart of all meaningful relationships is marriage. The curse hit us at the base of our most-needed relationship: "It is not good that the man should be alone" (Gen. 2:18). Man desperately needs a helper—someone with whom he can fulfill his deep drives and physical needs, and someone who can be his friend. Satan attacks the core of man's greatest need and makes it virtually impossible for him to build that needed relationship on his own. Then, along comes the sick world, spawned by Satan himself, and tells him that if he really wants to live it up, he should have an affair here and there, swap wives, be a swinger or a homosexual and be proud of it. The confusion gets worse and worse, and meaningful relationships become impossible.

Are You Buying the World's Fantasy or God's Reality?

Our society denies reality and extols fantasy. Think about the songs of our culture. They are about affairs, wild living, the perfect girl, and the perfect man, promising that the perfect relationship will make everything turn out the way we thought it should be. Singers promote ideas such as, "I've found the beautiful face, the attractive body, the wonderful personality; I'm going to finally have a relationship with no boredom, no unfaithfulness, no break-up, no pain, no loneliness, no leaving, no having to start all over again—and it's going to be that way until we die." That's all a dream. Worldly people are looking for a special relationship, but there's no way they are going to find one. So, sadly, our world lives with illusions and fantasies.

One fantasy is that if you really want to live it up, you've got to have super sex—which, in the world's view, is with a man or woman you're not married to. The fantasy of super sex is on the screen, in books, in magazines, in records—it's everywhere. There's another fantasy that someday "that perfect person" or "that wonderful relationship" will come and be so perfect that nothing could ever compare with it.

It's sad that our society lives with those fantasies, because they don't realize that the only place they're ever going to find reality is in the Word of God, by knowing Jesus Christ, by being filled with His Spirit, and by letting a relationship be what only God can make it. The fantasy about "that perfect someone" outside marriage will never happen. And all that talk about real sex, real fun, real living, and "doing your own thing" being outside your marriage is a lie. But because people in the world aren't willing to listen to God, they're not going to know the answers. The illusions are in the world, but the reality is in the Word of God.

Ephesians 5:22-33 is the greatest treatise on marriage ever written. Here we see marriage as it was before the Fall, where a wife submitted lovingly to her husband's care, protection, and leadership, and where a husband lovingly and sacrificially gave himself to meet every need his wife, whom he lifted up and exalted with all his heart. Now, if we're going to see that kind of relationship in our marriages, Christ must be at our center, and the Spirit of God must pervade us. In other words, once a person is "in Christ" (Eph. 1-3) and "filled with the Spirit" (Eph. 5:18), it becomes possible for a wife to submit to her husband and a husband to love his wife. The Christian marriage as God designed it and as Paul discusses it in Ephesians 5 is a reverse of the Fall. So the ultimate tragedy, then, is conflict in a Christian marriage, because it denies all the potential that God has placed there. If you are a believer, you have all the resources necessary to make your relationship all that God intended marriage to be before the Fall—at least as close as we can get to it.

Review

I. THE DUTY OF THE WIFE (vv. 22-24; see pp. 23-36, 43-53)

Lesson

II. THE DUTY OF THE HUSBAND (vv. 25-33)

Men, we are to love our wives. And according to verse 21 ("submitting yourselves one to another"), we submit to our wives by loving them. Keep in mind that our submission is mutual submission. The tendency of the man is to dominate the woman, to be chauvinistic, to be macho—and our society exalts that image. But that attitude is depraved and nothing more than a manifestation of human sinfulness.

Now the word Paul uses here for "love" is the Greek word *agapē*—the strongest, most intimate, far-reaching, comprehensive, fulfilling term for love. Yes, there is authority in a marriage. Yes, the husband is the head, and the wife is the one who follows. But verse 25 doesn't say, "Husbands, rule your wives," or, "Husbands, order your wives around," or, "Husbands, subject your wives," or, "Husbands, command your

wives, exercise authority over them, and dominate them."
Paul says, "Husbands, *love* your wives, even as Christ also
loved the church" (v. 25, emphasis added). How are we to love
our wives?

A. The Manner of Love (vv. 25-31)

Romans 5:8 says, "God commendeth his love toward us in
that, while we were yet sinners [as well as enemies, v. 10],
Christ died for us." Christ gave the greatest gift for the
most unworthy people—the contrast is incredible. He is
absolutely holy and righteous, untainted and unspotted.
He is without flaw. Yet this absolutely perfect One made
the absolutely ultimate sacrifice for the worst of sinners.
That is how Christ loved the church.

That's One!

There's a story about a newlywed couple, riding in a horse-drawn
carriage, headed for their honeymoon. Suddenly the horse bolted,
and the man said to the horse, "That's one!" They went a little
farther, and the horse bolted again. The man said, "That's two!" A
little farther the horse bolted again, and the man said, "That's
three!" He turned around, took out a gun, and shot the horse.
Shocked at what she had just witnessed, the new wife exclaimed,
"What have you done? What made you do that?" The man replied,
"That's one!"

Some people approach marriage on a one-two-three basis. If God
gave us only three chances, we'd all be in hell. An absolutely holy,
righteous God made the greatest, most magnanimous sacrifice for
the vilest of all people. Husbands, don't tell me about your wife's
problems. You're not as far removed from your wife as God was
from sinners, yet He loved you. Your wife may be a sinner, but so
are you. Don't lose that perspective.

I've heard men say, "Well, I just don't love her anymore." If that's
true, they are being disobedient to God's command. Husbands,
God commands us to love our wives.

Romans 8:35-39 tells us even more about the love of Christ:
"What shall separate us from the love of Christ? Shall tribu-

lation, or distress, or persecution, or famine, or nakedness, or peril, or sword? . . . I am persuaded that neither death, nor life, nor angels, nor principalities, nor powers, nor things present, nor things to come, nor height, nor depth, nor any other creation, shall be able to separate us from the love of God, which is in Christ Jesus, our Lord." Men, nothing can separate us from Christ's love, and we are to love our wives as Christ loves His church. That's a command of God. It's an act of your will. If you decide you're not going to do it, you won't, but if you decide to love her by the grace of God as Jesus loves the church, then no matter what happens, you'll love her.

A man once feared he was loving his wife too much. When a Christian asked him if he loved her as much as Christ loved the church, he answered, "No, not nearly as much." His friend replied, "Then you'd better love her more."

Three Practical Ways to Love Your Wife

1. Consideration

First Peter 3:7 says, "In like manner, ye husbands, dwell with them [wives] according to knowledge." If you're going to love your wife, you must be sensitive, understanding, and considerate. Women often say to me, "My husband never understands me. He doesn't know where I'm at. He's insensitive to my needs. We never talk. He doesn't know what I feel. He doesn't know what I'm thinking about. He doesn't understand my hurts." I hear that over and over again. It builds a wall in marriages. When Peter said, "Dwell with them according to knowledge," he was saying, "Be sensitive, be understanding, feel what she feels." It isn't what you get out of marriage; it's what you give that God is after.

2. Chivalry

Peter continues in verse 7, "Giving honor unto the wife, as unto the weaker vessel." In other words, husbands, realize that physically and emotionally you are stronger than your wives. Whatever happened to chivalry? Whatever happened to the custom of opening the car door for your wife? You may be fifteen feet down the driveway while she still has one foot out the door! Husbands, practice chivalry with your wives.

3. Communion

First Peter 3:7 says, "As being heirs together of the grace of life, that your prayers be not hindered." The phrase "the grace of life" is like the hot fudge on a sundae. Marriage is the hot fudge on the top of life. And since you've inherited marriage, commune together, talk together, and share together. There's a spiritual thought here too: "That your prayers be not hindered." You need to share your spiritual lives.

God has given us the ingredients to make marriage work. He can reverse the curse when we're in Christ and filled with the Spirit. Husbands, when we look at our wives and determine in our hearts that we're going to love them as Christ loved the church, making great sacrifices for them—even if they are unworthy—and being considerate, chivalrous, and willing to commune with them on a spiritual level, I'll promise you one thing: marriage *will* turn out to be the hot fudge on the sundae. It will be everything God ever make it to be, and you'll give a legacy to your children that will not only have an effect on their marriages but also in the marriages of generations to follow.

Focusing on the Facts

1. How is marriage usually portrayed in movies, books, and television (see p. 58)?
2. According to Genesis 2:18, why did God create a suitable helper for Adam (see p. 58)?
3. Describe the perfect relationship that Adam and Eve originally had (see pp. 58-59).
4. Cite four reasons for marriage (see p. 59).
5. Why did the serpent approach Eve rather than Adam? Explain the reversal of roles that took place as the woman sinned (see p. 59).
6. What are four elements of the curse (see p. 60)?
7. Describe how to have a marriage that works (see p. 61).
8. How have men abused women through the media (see p. 62)?

9. Besides the curse, what else makes it difficult for marriage to work? What were some of the manifestations of corrupt human relationships in Genesis (see pp. 62-63)?
10. What does society extol that makes marriage even more difficult (see p. 63)?
11. What does every man desperately need (see p. 63)?
12. Our society denies _____ and extols _____ (see p. 64).
13. What is the ultimate tragedy among relationships? Why (see p. 65)?
14. How does Paul command husbands to treat their wives (Eph. 5:25; see pp. 65-66)?
15. What is to be the standard of a husband's love for his wife (Eph. 5:25; see p. 66)?
16. Explain how Christ loved the church (see pp. 66-67).
17. How are husbands to love their wives according to 1 Peter 3:7 (see pp. 67-68)?
18. What must husbands realize about their wives' physical and emotional makeup (see p. 67)?

Pondering the Principles

1. What is shaping your expectations for marriage: the world's fantasies or God's realities? Do television and magazines determine the kind of clothes you wear, the activities you participate in, and the relationships you have? If so, realize that they have established false expectations based on worldly standards of superficial and temporary value. Many times, unrealized expectations can be a source of conflict in a marriage. Sit down with your spouse or fiancé and list the expectations that each of you has for the other. Next, determine which of those have a biblical foundation. In that way you can resolve potential conflicts before they start. Focus on what you can give to your partner rather than what you can get. By doing so, you will help to prevent any expectations from not being met.

2. Husband, have you ever felt you don't love your wife anymore? Is the attraction you once had for her waning? If so, confess your lack of love, realizing that you are commanded to sacrificially love her as an act of your will. You may not feel romantic about her, but that response will come if you commit yourself to doing what is right. If you work in an office with women, recog-

nize that a lack of love for your spouse might lead to an increased attraction to someone at work. Calculate the number of hours you spend with women at work and those you spend with your wife. Do you see a danger of communicating better with the women at work than with your spouse? Do you find yourself sharing intimate things with them that you don't even communicate to your wife? Sin is deceiving and can subtly entice you into pursuing relationships that have the appearance of being fulfilling but will actually break down the quality of love you should be investing in your wife. Read Proverbs 5:15-23 and 6:20-35. You may not currently be faced with the temptation to commit adultery, but prepare yourself for the appropriate response to that possibility.

3. Of the three practical ways to love your wife mentioned on pages 67-68, in which area are you weakest? Write down on a card the things you can be doing to strengthen that area. Every morning and night during the next week, read that card as you seek to establish good habits of practical loving.

5
The Divine Pattern for Marriage—Part 5
The Husband's Priorities

Outline

Introduction
A. The Decadence of the Last Days
  1. Its certainty
  2. Its characteristics
    a) Self-love
    b) Rebellion in the family
    c) Lack of normal familial love
    d) Attacks directed against the home
B. The Difficulty of Marriage

Review
I. The Duty of the Wife (vv. 22-24)

Lesson
II. The Duty of the Husband (vv. 25-33)
  A. The Manner of Love (vv. 25-31)
    1. Sacrificial love (v. 25)
      a) Its example
      b) Its essence
        (1) Properly characterized
        (2) Predominantly corrupted
      c) Its exhortation
    2. Purifying love (vv. 26-27)
      a) The Lord's purification of His church
        (1) Positional cleansing
        (2) Daily cleansing
      b) The husband's purification of his wife
    3. Caring love (vv. 28-30)

4. Unbreakable love (v. 31)
   a) "For this cause"
   b) "Leave"
   c) "Joined"
   B. The Motive of Love (vv. 32-33)

Introduction

The Seven Ages of the Married Cold

Several years ago, the *Saturday Evening Post* published an article entitled "The Seven Ages of the Married Cold." It revealed the reaction of a husband to his wife's colds during their first seven years of marriage. It went something like this:

The first year: "Sugar dumpling, I'm really worried about my baby girl. You've got a bad sniffle, and there's no telling about these things with all this strep throat going around. I'm putting you in the hospital this afternoon for a general checkup and a good rest. I know the food's lousy, but I'll be bringing your meals in from Rossini's. I've already got it all arranged with the floor superintendent."

The second year: "Listen, darling, I don't like the sound of that cough. I called Doc Miller and asked him to rush over here. Now you go to bed like a good girl, please? Just for papa."

The third year: "Maybe you'd better lie down, honey; nothing like a little rest when you feel lousy. I'll bring you something to eat. Have you got any canned soup?"

The fourth year: "Now look, dear, be sensible. After you've fed the kids, washed the dishes, and finished the floor, you'd better lie down."

The fifth year: "Why don't you take a couple of aspirin?"

The sixth year: "I wish you'd just gargle or something, instead of sitting around all evening barking like a seal!"

The seventh year: "For Pete's sake, stop sneezing! Are you trying to give me pneumonia?"

The decline of marriage as seen through the common cold. A funny look at a not-so-funny reality.

Psychologist Carl Rogers in his book *Becoming Partners: Marriage and Its Alternatives*, said, "To me it seems that we are living in an important and uncertain age, the institution of marriage is most assuredly in an uncertain state. If 50 to 75 percent of Ford or General Motors' cars completely fell apart within the early part of their lifetimes as automobiles, drastic steps would be taken. We have no such well organized way of dealing with our social institutions, so people are groping, more or less blindly, to find alternatives to marriage (which is certainly less than 50 percent successful). Living together without marriage, living in communes, extensive child care centers, serial monogamy (with one divorce after another), the women's liberation movement to establish the woman as a person in her own right, new divorce laws which do away with the concept of guilt—these are all groping toward some new form of man-woman relationship for the future. It would take a bolder man than I to predict what will emerge" [New York: Delacorte, 1972], p. 11).

Carl Rogers admits that in trying those alternatives to marriage people are "groping" for a new definition of man-woman relationships. But we don't need to grope; all we need to do is to go back to the Creator to find out how these relationships ought to work. After all, God made us—He must know.

Carl Rogers said it would take a bolder man than he to predict what will happen to marriage. The Bible itself predicts what will happen in 2 Timothy 3.

A. The Decadence of the Last Days

1. Its certainty

   Second Timothy 3:1 says, "This know, also, that in the last days perilous times shall come." Then verse 13, which is a summary of those perilous times, says, "Evil men and seducers shall become worse and worse, deceiving, and being deceived." In other words, it's going to get worse—not better.

2. Its characteristics

   a) Self-love

   Verse 2 says, "Men shall be lovers of their own selves." The first characteristic of the last days noted

73

here is that there will be an overwhelming sense of self-centeredness, selfishness, self-absorption, self-indulgence, and self-satisfaction. People will be looking at what they can get. There will be a time in the last days when men will become more and more in love with themselves.

b) Rebellion in the family

Another characteristic of the last days is mentioned at the end of verse 2: disobedience to parents. Children will lose their sense of respect and lack of proper perspective of authority. There will be rebellion in the family, and no obedience will be shown to parents. We're seeing this today. Juvenile crime is increasing at a rate beyond comprehension. Disobedience to parents is part of the problem, but with day-care centers, separations of families, and so forth, I'm not sure that children even comprehend, in many cases, what a parent is and what their role is supposed to be.

c) Lack of normal familial love

Another interesting characteristic of the last days is in verse 3: "Without natural affection." This phrase in the Greek test, *astorgoi*, comes from *storgē*, which means "familial affection." The *a*, when put in front of a word, means "without." Literally, then, *astorgoi* means "without familial affection."

d) Attacks directed against the home

Verse 6 says, "For of this sort are they who creep into houses, and lead captive silly women laden with sins, led away with various lusts." The home is going to become fair game for every con man and sexual pervert. It's all going to come crashing down on the home, God's basic unit of human society.

B. The Difficulty of Marriage

In our last lesson we saw that marriage is difficult because of the curse of God (see pp. 58-62), the corruptions of Satan (see pp. 62-63), and the confusion of society (see pp. 63-65). Now, add to those the characteristics of the last days as seen in 2 Timothy 3, and it becomes apparent that there's little hope for marriage—at least on human terms. But there is a way we can have relationships that are designed and fulfilled the way God intended them, which brings us back to Ephesians 5.

Review

I. THE DUTY OF THE WIFE (vv. 22-24; see pp. 23-36, 43-53)

Lesson

II. THE DUTY OF THE HUSBAND (vv. 25-33)

Many times I've heard people teach this passage and say, "The wives are to submit, and the husbands are to rule." But this passage doesn't say that. It says wives are to be submitting, and husbands are to be loving. You can't forget the mutuality that is present there. Yes, the husband has the leadership, and he is the stronger vessel, but that doesn't mean he is to rule the wife and lord it over her. That is what the curse does—and we're trying to get marriage back to a co-regency, as God intended it before the Fall. Verse 25 says, "Husbands, love your wives, even as Christ also loved the church, and gave himself for it." Dying for someone is the most magnanimous act of submission possible. Husbands are to be submitting to their wives as well. There is beautiful mutuality (cf. 1 Cor. 7:4, 33-34). The husband is to love his wife; that is his act of submission.

A. The Manner of Love (vv. 25-31; see pp. 66-68)

"Husbands, love your wives, even as Christ also loved the church." The standard is infinitely high. However, the text isn't talking about the full capacity of divine love; it's talking about the factors involved in the kind of love Christ manifested. Obviously we cannot match God's love in quantity, or even in quality, but we can love in *kind*. We

75

may not possess the ocean, but we can have a little of it in our bucket.

1. Sacrificial love (v. 25)

> "As Christ also loved the church, and gave [lit., "gave up"] himself for it."

a) Its example

When Jesus Christ came into the world, He loved the church. In fact, He loved the church before the foundation of the world in eternity past. And He loved us enough to leave heaven, come to earth, take on a human form, be spit on and mocked, crowned with a crown of thorns, nailed to a cross, abused, and have a spear thrust into His side. He loved the church enough to die. That's sacrificial love. And it is sacrificial love that is to mark the love of a husband for his wife. When Christ gave up His prerogative to be equal with God and chose to come to earth in the form of a servant, He was acting in sacrificial love.

b) Its essence

(1) Properly characterized

Sacrificial love has nothing to do with whether it's deserved or not. There wasn't a soul on the globe that deserved what Christ did for them. When our names were written in the Lamb's Book of Life before the foundation of the world, when God by His sovereign love placed us in the Body of Christ, and when we were chosen to be His children, it was not because we were deserving. Sacrificial love is undeserved. God is not rescuing people who deserve rescue; He is saving those who don't deserve it because it's His nature to love. An inferior love gives only to those who earn the right to receive it. But God's love is given to those who don't have the right to earn it.

(2) Predominantly corrupted

> The world loves with an object-oriented love. So if the object is desirable, the world says, "I love you." When people pick a partner, they look around and say, "There's a nice one. I'll love that one," or, "Forget that one." Or they go through a group of people and say, "I don't care for those people; they aren't worthy of my love. They don't live up to my expectations. They don't fit into my little group. But those people—oh, I love them." Everything depends upon the form of an object or its personality. We have an object-oriented attraction.

God's love is different. God doesn't expect the object to be worthy; it's His nature to love. That's the difference. John 3:16 says, "For God so *loved* the world" (emphasis added). If God was going to love anything, and it was a matter of being attractive, it wouldn't have been the world. The world hated God, but God loved the world. It's not the object that defines God's love; it is His nature to love.

c) Its exhortation

When Paul says in Ephesians 5:25, "Husbands, love your wives," he's not saying "love her because she deserves it"; he's saying "love her even if she doesn't deserve it. Love her enough to die for her, whether she's worthy of dying for or not." We are commanded to love our wives. It isn't an issue of attraction; it's an issue of a binding commandment from God. However, I believe you will become greatly attracted to what you choose to love.

Sacrificial love is undeserved, yet it goes to the furthest extremity, as exemplified in Christ. It says, "You don't deserve anything, but I'll give you everything. You don't deserve anything, but I'll die for you. You don't even deserve My best, but I'll give you My life." And Paul is saying that we are to say to our wives, "You may not deserve all those things, you may be a sinner, and you may not be all that you

77

could be, but that is never the issue. I love you and commit myself to you, even if you are the least deserving. And I will give you everything I have—even to the point of dying for you."

Is Love an Emotion?

Love, as God defines it, is not an emotion. The world says, "When the feeling stops, the love is over." That kind of love creates serial monogamy; it's not the love of the Bible. The love of the Bible is not a feeling; it is an act of selfless sacrifice. Anyone with a need is worthy of it.

Jesus washed the disciples' feet (John 13). Why? Because they deserved it? No; they were arguing about who would be the greatest in the kingdom. They were on an ego trip; they were selfish, self-centered, self-indulgent, and absolutely insensitive to the fact that Jesus was going to the cross. And in their self-indulgence they refused to wash each other's feet. Finally, Jesus stepped down and washed their feet. And when He was done He said to them, "A new commandment I give unto you, that ye love one another; as I have loved you" (v. 34). How had He loved them? Certainly not by feeling emotional. If anything, He probably felt pain because of their selfishness and sorrow because of their indifference. But in His sorrow and pain, He washed their feet. Love doesn't act out what it feels; it does what is right. Where there is a need, love acts. And in a marriage, it isn't a matter of whether your partner deserves your love; it's a matter of sharing love because it is right.

John 3:16 doesn't say, "For God so loved the world that He felt emotional about it." God didn't look at this world and say, "I just can't resist them; I've got to get them in heaven. They're terrific." There wasn't one thing in us that was deserving. We were enemies; we hated God; we were sinful and vile, but God loved us anyway. And He loved us so much, He gave Himself.

In Acts 20:28 Paul says, "The church of God, which he hath purchas:d with his own blood." We were so rotten, He had to die to claim us. We were so far gone, He had to give His life to rescue us. And Paul basically says in Ephesians 5:25, "That's the way I want you to love your wives." It's not emotion. Now, if you commit yourself to love you may become emotional, but you must first realize that love is always a verb. Love always acts, meets needs, does whatever has to be done, and reaches out.

Husbands, you will never know how to love until you've sacrificed yourself, crucified yourself, and died to yourself. Paul says that love "seeketh not its own" (1 Cor. 13:5). As long as you're looking for what you can get out of marriage, you will never know what it is to love your wife as Christ loved the church.

Ask yourself: When is the last time I made a sacrifice for my wife? When is the last time I sacrificed myself for my wife? When is the last time I came close to actually being willing to die for my wife? When is the last time, when we both wanted to do different things, that I said, "Honey, I think what you want to do is what we ought to do"? When is the last time I set aside my own carefully laid out plans to do what my wife suddenly decided she wanted to do? The whole heart of the matter is dying to self.

Is He or Isn't He?

There are many men who want to be spiritual leaders. They want to be preachers, teachers, elders, or deacons—and they want to be pious. But if you want to know whether a man is genuine, check out his home. Find out the last time he made a sacrifice for his wife. Find out whether he would die for her. Find out whether he would give up everything he has to meet her needs. If you do that, you'll find out if he is genuine. If true spiritual life isn't a reality in the home, then it's a facade on the outside. You may be playing spiritual giant, but if you're not sacrificially giving up yourself for the needs of your wife, you've missed the point. Love meets needs; worthiness isn't an issue.

Husbands, we need to die to self. Our world tells us: "Be the macho man. Be the big shot. Don't let anyone step on your territory. Fight back; you deserve more. Build up your identity. Be somebody. Grab all the gusto. Live for the moment." But the Bible says, "Crucify yourself"—the opposite of what the world says. Somewhere along the line, if you're going to love your wife as God says you should, and if you're going to love her as Christ (who was willing to die) loved the church, then you're going to have to make a sacrifice for her.

2. Purifying love (vv. 26-27)

"That he might sanctify and cleanse it with the washing of water by the word; that he might present it to himself a glorious church, not having spot, or wrinkle, or any such thing; but that it should be holy and without blemish."

a) The Lord's purification of His church

Christ loved the church. He wanted to cleanse it and purify it. This teaches us a basic truth: when you love someone, his purity is your goal. No one loves something and then wants to defile it. Christ loved His church, so He wanted to purify His people.

(1) Positional cleansing

When you are saved, the Lord Jesus Christ cleanses every sin you committed and will commit. The Bible says that Christ has "forgiven you all trespasses" (Col. 2:13). The moment you opened your heart and invited Christ in, He cleansed you so absolutely that "though your sins be as scarlet, they shall be as white as snow; though they be red like crimson, they shall be as wool" (Isa. 1:18). He has removed your sin "as far as the east is from the west" (Ps. 103:12), and then cast them "into the depths of the sea" (Mic. 7:19). He says, "I will remember their sin no more" (Jer. 31:34). When you were saved, He made you absolutely pure so that you can enter into the presence of God covered in His absolute righteousness: "For he hath made him, who knew no sin, to be sin for us, that we might be made the righteousness of God in him" (2 Cor. 5:21). When you were saved, you were absolutely purified. Past, present, and future, every sin was done away with, and forever you'll be pure.

(2) Daily cleansing

In John 13:10 Jesus essentially says to Peter, "He that is bathed doesn't need to take another bath

80

[Gk., *louō*]; you just need your feet washed [Gk., *niptō*]." In the Orient, a man would get up in the morning and bathe himself. Then, as he went through the day and his feet got dirty, he would wash them as they needed it. The idea is that when you came to Christ, you were totally cleansed, positionally, before God. But every day you walk through the world and get your feet dusty; so Jesus keeps washing your feet. There is, then, the need for both a total positional cleansing and a continuous daily cleansing. When you were saved, all your sins were washed away; yet 1 John 1:9 says He keeps on cleansing us from all sin. You were bathed once, and you're continuously kept pure.

b) The husband's purification of his wife

Did you know that marrying someone purifies her by taking her out of the world and apart from the past? Whatever relationships she may have had, whatever indulgences she may have had, or whatever other things she may have done, marriage sets her apart and purifies her. And not only in the act of marriage do you purify that person, but every day you live. If you really love your wife, you'll seek that which keeps her feet clean from the dust of the world. If you love your wife, you will do everything in your power to maintain her holiness, her virtue, her righteousness, and her purity every day you live. You'll never put her in a compromising situation where she would become angered, because that's a sin. You would never induce an argument out of her, because that's a sin. You would do nothing to defile her. You would never let her see anything, expose her to anything, or let her indulge in anything that would bring any impurity into her life. Love always seeks to purify.

Here's some advice for women who aren't married. If a man comes along and tells you he loves you and then tries to take away your virtue, that is not love. Don't ever believe that definition of love. Love lifts up, purifies, exalts, honors, makes holy, and sanctifies.

Husband, if you love your wife, seek to lift her up, draw her to God, pour virtue into her life, and make her, in every possible way, like Christ. Husband, that's your spiritual responsibility—you're the purifier.

Look again at verse 26: Christ sanctifies and cleanses the church "with the washing of water by the word." It is the Word of God that keeps us pure (cf. John 15:3). It was God's Word that redeemed us, and it is God's Word that keeps us clean. Men, you have the responsibility in your home to apply to your wife every purifying influence that will make her holy. Do everything you can to ensure her purity.

Further, in verse 27, Paul says that the Lord wants to present to Himself "a glorious church [Gk., *endoxon*, "an intense splendidness"], not having spot [Gk., *spilon*, "stain"], or wrinkle [Gk., *rhutida*, "flaw"], or any such thing; but that it should be holy and without blemish." Men, that is how we are to deal with our wives. Don't ever do anything in your life that will lead your wife into any illicit thought or relationship. Don't ever do anything that would cause her to look to someone else for fulfillment. Fulfill your love to her so she is purified, sanctified, and lifted up to God—that's your responsibility.

3. Caring love (vv. 28-30)

    a) "So ought men to love their wives as their own bodies. He that loveth his wife loveth himself" (v. 28)

Men, we spend a lot of time on our bodies by jogging, exercising, eating the right foods, and wearing nice clothes. After all, a Christian's body is the temple of the Holy Spirit. We certainly don't want to mar it, so we take good care of it. What Paul is saying here is this: "Look, you ought to love your wives as you love your own body."

Again, notice that love is not an emotion. When your body has needs, you meet them. Your wife also has needs, and you're to meet them too. And even though love is not an emotion, I believe that emotion can follow the meeting of a need. As you meet the needs of your wife, it's going to change your emotional response.

b) "For no man ever yet hated his own flesh, but nourisheth and cherisheth it, even as the Lord the church" (v. 29).

Does the Lord care for the church? Does He take care of everything we need? The Bible doesn't say, "My God shall supply most of your needs . . . if you don't get too picky or make too many demands." Philippians 4:19 says, "My God shall supply *all* your need according to his riches in glory by Christ Jesus" (emphasis added). If you need love, or joy, or peace, or strength, or wisdom, or anything else, He will give it to you. You will never do without what you need to fulfill His will.

Men, God is saying that we are to give our wives every single thing they need. Now, maybe she needs to understand the difference between needs and wants. If so, help her to do that. But, what she needs, you must supply. Don't forget that. The man is the provider, the protector, and the preserver. He is the one who grants the resources. We are to care for our wives as we care for our own bodies—as Christ cares for the church. Something is wrong if you look at your wife as a cook, baby-sitter, clothes washer, and sex partner—and nothing more. She is a God-given treasure to be cared for, cherished, and nourished.

(1) "Nourisheth"

This word in verse 29 is a fantastic word. It is the Greek word *ektrephō*, which means "to nourish" or "to feed." Primarily, it's used in reference to nurturing or raising children. It simply means "to mature." Men, we're called to nurture our wives,

83

to bring them to maturity, and to provide for their needs. Also, because *ektrephō* literally means "to feed," I believe this reiterates the principle that the man is to be the breadwinner, the provider.

What did you provide for your salvation? Nothing. What resources do you provide to live the Christian life? Nothing. As Christ provides for the church, so a husband should provide for his wife. We're to nourish, feed, nurture, bring up, and mature our wives. We are to be their preservers, their saviors, and their protectors.

(2) "Cherisheth"

This word literally means "to soften or warm with body heat." It is used to describe a bird sitting on her nest (cf. Deut. 22:6). Husbands are to literally provide a secure, warm, soft place as a provision for their wives. Husbands are to provide the security. Don't shove your wife out into the cold, hard, cruel world. We are to provide our wives with a nest, a security, a place of warmth, and a place of nourishment. Again, this idea is relinquished in the case of the working mother. She should not be the one who nourishes and feeds; she should receive that provision.

In the curse in Genesis 3, the wife was cursed in two areas: (1) she would have pain in child bearing, and (2) she would have a hard time submitting to her husband (see pp. 59-62)—but both areas are centered in the home. Now notice where the curse on the man comes. He's cursed in that he will have to till the ground and work in the sweat of his brow to provide bread for his family. From the beginning it was assumed that the woman would be home with the children, meeting the needs of her family, and the man would be out working to provide for those needs. That is God's design. As Christ provides for the church, so the husband is to provide for his wife that which nourishes her and provides security.

84

c) "For we are members of his body, of his flesh, and of his bones" (v. 30)

You may ask, "Why does Christ care for us as He does? Why does He meet every need we have? Why is He so wonderfully caring? Why did He go through all the things He went through to provide everything for us as a sympathetic, loving, faithful, High Priest?" The answer is in verse 30: we are members of His body—His flesh and His bone. We're one with Him. Not to provide for us would be not to provide for Himself. We are one with Christ.

(1) "He that is joined unto the Lord is one spirit" (1 Cor. 6:17)

(2) "I am crucified with Christ: nevertheless I live; yet not I, but Christ liveth in me" (Gal. 2:20)

(3) "For by one Spirit were we all baptized into one body" (1 Cor. 12:13)

Because we are one with Christ, He will meet our needs.

Husband, your wife is one with you. Not to meet her needs is to commit spiritual suicide, because you are one. People who violate their marriage destroy themselves.

The grace of God is amazing. God incorporates us into a body and says, "As Christ cares for His body, the church, and as a man cares for his own physical body, so is a husband to care for his wife—meeting her needs and providing all that is necessary." Men, God has a high view of women. They are to be exalted, honored, and lifted up. We're to submit to meeting their needs —even if we must die doing it—and cause them to be pure, honored, holy, and sanctified.

4. Unbreakable love (v. 31)

"For this cause shall a man leave his father and mother, and shall be joined unto his wife, and they two shall be one flesh."

That is a direct quote from Genesis 2:24. It is nothing new. People say, "You've got to get the Bible up to date. Times have changed." But that is a direct quote. The Bible was written over a period of 1500 years; nothing has changed. Thousands of years back, when God first created man, He said, "Therefore shall a man leave his father and his mother, and shall cleave unto his wife; and they shall be one flesh." Genesis 2:24 appears in Ephesians 5:31. Nothing has changed. It's the same standard; marriage is an unbreakable, indivisible union.

a) "For this cause"

Why is marriage unbreakable? Because marriage partners become one—and they cannot be separated. Some people think that a Christian can lose his salvation. But if that were true, Christ would have to cut off a part of His own body. As members of His body, we cannot be separated from Him. The point is this: the body is indivisible and cannot be cut apart. It is one flesh and one bone. Because of that, when you marry you are to leave your father and mother, join your wife, and become one flesh. It becomes an indivisible union, because you can't divide one.

b) "Leave"

The Greek word *leipō* means "to leave." But the word used here is an intensified form, *kataleipō,* and means "to abandon completely." Married couples run into a big problem if they don't leave their mothers and fathers completely when they step into the marriage relationship. That doesn't mean they shouldn't talk to their parents anymore; it means they need to have a conscious understanding of the new relationship that has been formed.

c) "Joined"

The Greek word used here is *proskollaō*, an intensification of the word *kollaō*, which means "to connect up." *Proskollaō* means "to glue together." The idea is that you are to leave, and then you are to glue the new relationship together. It is a new relationship, absolutely unbreakable. Two become one.

What Does God Think of Divorce?

Do you want to know what God thinks of divorce? Malachi 2:16 says, "The Lord, the God of Israel, saith that he hateth putting away [divorce]." That's how God feels about divorce. And by the way, God hasn't changed His mind, because in Malachi 3:6 God says, "I am the Lord, I change not." God has always hated divorce; He hates it now, and He'll always hate it. There's no divorce He doesn't hate. You may say, "But my divorce was justified. My partner committed adultery." God still hates it. He hates divorce on any terms or on any condition. He forgives it, but He still hates it. Now, He hates a lot of things He forgives, but that doesn't change the fact that He hates divorce.

I've had women say to me, "I'm finally going to divorce my husband. We haven't gotten along for years, but he finally committed adultery. Now I can divorce him." I usually say to them, "You know what? God hates divorce. And not only that, God hates your satisfaction in considering your divorce justified." Don't be glad for evil. God hates divorce.

Should You Divorce Your Partner in the Case of Adultery?

When God designed marriage, He designed it to be like a body: indivisible, two becoming one. But many spouses aren't willing to forgive their partners when they sin. If Jesus divorced us every time we sinned, where would we be? Since we're to love our wives the way Christ loves the church, how many times are we to forgive? How many times has Christ forgiven you? Should you cast your wife off if she is unfaithful? Did Christ cast you off when you were unfaithful? Did God cast Israel off when Israel committed adultery? Israel committed and still commits many adulteries, but some day God will recover Israel and give her the kingdom. The church, too, has sinned again and again; but Jesus does not cast us off. He keeps on cleansing us. If your spouse sins, your response should be forgiveness.

That kind of forgiveness is illustrated in the life of Hosea. God told Hosea to marry a woman who was a prostitute. Then He told him to keep forgiving her for her continued prostitutions. And Hosea did—he kept on forgiving her again and again. Finally, God restored their marriage into a wonderful blessing. There was true love, and she was purified. Then God said to Hosea, "That was an illustration of My relationship with Israel. I love Israel. She is My wife, and she commits adultery after adultery; but I'll never put her away. I still love her." And in the end, ultimately, He's going to regather that wayward wife back into the fold.

Look at the church. Jesus loves the church. And even though the church is unfaithful and sinful, He never puts us away. He keeps on forgiving us (1 John 1:9).

B. The Motive of Love (vv. 32-33)

Ephesians 5:32 says, "This is a great mystery [a secret from the past], but I speak concerning Christ and the church." You may ask, "Why is it important to love like that? Why is it important that marriage be based on those principles?" Because it is a picture of the church. This magnificent picture was a mystery, never known in the past, but now revealed. The sacredness of the church is wed to the sacredness of marriage; so by your marriage, you are either a symbol or a denial of Christ and His church.

Because marriage is so sacred, Paul says in verse 33, "Nevertheless, let every one of you in particular so love his wife even as himself; and the wife, see that she reverence her husband." If we would learn, in Christ and the power of the Spirit, to base the marriage relationship on God's principles, there would be an end to much anxiety. Approach your marriage God's way. And watch God pour out so much blessing you won't even be able to receive it all!

Focusing on the Facts

1. Describe the characteristics that will work against the family in the last days (2 Tim. 3:2-3, 6; see pp. 73-75).
2. How is the husband supposed to express his submission to his wife (see pp. 75-76)?
3. Do we deserve God's sacrificial love? Explain your answer (see pp. 76-77).
4. How does the world's love compare to God's love (see p. 77)?
5. You will become greatly _____ to what you _____ to love (see p. 77).
6. Define biblical love. Who is worthy to receive it? How did Jesus demonstrate it in John 13 (see p. 78)?
7. Love doesn't act out what it _____; it does what is _____ (see p. 78).
8. What must a husband do before he can properly love his wife (see p. 79)?
9. Because Christ loved the church, what did He seek to do? What should be your goal with regard to someone you love (see pp. 79-80)?
10. In what two ways are Christians cleansed from their sins? Explain (see pp. 80-81).
11. Why is premarital sex not an expression of true love (see p. 82)?
12. How do we show that our bodies are important to us? How does that relate to a husband's loving his wife, according to Ephesians 5:28-29? How does the Lord care for the church according to Philippians 4:19 (see p. 83)?
13. Why is Christ so willing to provide for the needs of Christians (see p. 85)?
14. How is the command about marriage in Genesis 2:24 evidence that the standards for marriage haven't changed (see p. 86)?
15. What is one of the biggest problems newly married couples might experience with their parents? What does Ephesians 5:31 command them to do (see pp. 86-87)?
16. What does God think of divorce? Has He changed His mind on that issue? Support your answers with Scripture (see p. 87).
17. If your spouse sins, what should be your response (see p. 88)?
18. Explain how Hosea is an illustration of God's forgiving love toward Israel (see p. 88).
19. Why is it important for marriage to be based on biblical principles (see pp. 88-89)?

Pondering the Principles

1. As long as you are looking for what you can get out of your marriage, you will never be able to fully give yourself to your spouse. Husbands, when was the last time you made a sacrifice for your wife by submitting to her needs and desires? Although your time may be valuable and your funds limited, what tangible expressions of love can you give your wife that will demonstrate how highly you value her as your life partner?

2. Men, if you love a woman, you should do everything in your power to preserve her purity. Do you ever encourage her to compromise her spiritual or moral standards? Or do you take advantage of the fact that she hasn't established any standards yet? What are you doing to draw her closer to God and to make her life more virtuous? Recognizing your natural concern for your own body and the fact that it is the temple of the Holy Spirit, make sure that you care for your wife with at least the same amount of zeal.

3. A symptom of a deteriorating relationship is a fault-finding attitude. If you are hoping that your partner will sin so you can justify a divorce, your attitude is totally wrong (see pp. 87-88). How many times have you sinned and been forgiven by God? Has God, in effect, divorced you? Paul tells us that nothing can "separate us from the love of God, which is in Christ Jesus" (Rom. 8:39). If an infinitely holy God keeps His promises to His children, who are undeserving of His love, we should be faithful to the one we have promised to love and care for until death. If you sense a growing separation in your marital relationship, pray that God would help you determine its cause and would empower you to build your marriage into one that honors and pleases Him.

6
The Divine Pattern for the Family—Part 1
Understanding the Issues

Outline

Introduction
A. The Source of the Attack on the Family
  1. God's plan
     a) The message of God
        (1) The theology
        (2) The response
     b) The mechanics for passing it on
        (1) Personal commitment
        (2) Parental communication
           (*a*) In speech
           (*b*) In symbols
           (*c*) In surroundings
  2. Satan's resistance
B. The Strategy of the Attack on the Family
  1. Fathers attacked
  2. Mothers attacked
  3. Children attacked
     a) Abandoned at home
     b) Influenced by TV
        (1) Violent role models
        (2) Godless morality
        (3) Stifled communication
     c) Raised by day-care centers
     d) Abused according to statistics
C. The Specifics of the Attack on the Family
  1. The curse of sin
  2. The failure of parents

3. The emergence of humanistic philosophy
   a) The International Year of the Child
      (1) Its source
      (2) Its efforts
   b) The Child's Bill of Rights
      (1) Liberation from traditional moral values
      (2) Liberation from parental authority
      (3) Liberation from discrimination
      (4) Liberation from nationalism and patriotism

Lesson
 I. The Submission of the Child (vv. 1-3)
II. The Submission of the Parents (v. 4)

Introduction

We now come to Ephesians 6:1-4, and our subject is the family. However, before we look specifically at the text, I want to give you a picture of what is going on around us in our world, so that you can better understand the importance of this text.

A. The Source of the Attack on the Family

Satan is attacking the family. We have already seen some of the ways he attacks the husband-wife relationship. In the aftermath of that attack, the family pays a tremendous price. For example, only 7 percent of Americans currently live in what we know as a normal family, where the father is the breadwinner and the mother is the homemaker (Ellen Goodman, "The Eruption of a Now-Styled Family Feud," *Los Angeles Times*, 25 June 1978). That is a dramatic statistic, indicating that we have moved a long way from the divine plan God established for the family. The family is being attacked by Satan.

1. God's plan

When God originally called out Israel as a people, He established that they be His witnesses. The nation of Israel was not an end in itself; it was a means to an end. God did not call Israel to be a bucket to receive all of His blessings, but a channel through which He could pass

His blessings to the world. Israel was to communicate the truth about God to the world.

a) The message of God

(1) The theology

"Hear, O Israel: the Lord our God is one Lord" (Deut. 6:4). This was the standard message, the basic heart of God's truth—the great statement that there is only one God. And it was to be passed on to the world.

(2) The response

"Thou shalt love the Lord thy God with all thine heart, and with all thy soul, and with all thy might" (v. 5). That is to be the human response to the reality of God.

b) The mechanics for passing it on

(1) Personal commitment

"These words, which I command thee this day, shall be in thine heart" (v. 6). The first key to passing on God's message to the world was that they had to make a personal commitment to love the Lord their God with all their heart, soul, and might. Once they made that commitment, there was a second step.

(2) Parental communication

"Thou shalt teach them diligently unto thy children" (v. 7). That is God's plan for passing on the truth about Himself—from parent to child. As a child matures, he becomes a parent to the next generation, and so on. How are God's truths to be communicated?

(*a*) In speech

> "And shalt talk of them when thou sittest in thine house, and when thou walkest by the way, and when thou liest down, and when thou risest up" (v. 7). Godly words were to be flowing out of their mouths. They were to be constantly speaking about the things of God.

(*b*) In symbols

> "Thou shalt bind them for a sign upon thine hand, and they shall be as frontlets between thine eyes" (v. 8). Even when there was silence, there was to be a visible commitment to the law of God. Here it was symbolized in what they wore.

(*c*) In surroundings

> "Thou shalt write them upon the posts of thy house, and on thy gates" (v. 9). Even when the parents weren't home, their children were to see the law of God written all over the house.

The children were to see God's Word throughout the house in their parents' absence; they were to see it symbolized in what their parents wore; and they were to hear it when their parents opened their mouths. The law of God was to be passed on so that godliness and righteousness could move from one generation to the next.

2. Satan's resistance

From the beginning, Satan has tried to upset the plan of God. To accomplish that, he plans to undermine the righteous seed. He wants to destroy the family by disrupting it, removing the children, and creating quarrels so that family life becomes chaotic. He uses divorces, separations, adulteries, fornications, and whatever else he can to fracture the family so it cannot do what God intends it to do.

B. The Strategy of the Attack on the Family

1. Fathers attacked

In many cases, fathers have abandoned their God-given role. A leading secular psychologist from the Menninger Clinic, Harold Voth, has written a provocative book called *The Castrated Family*. He presents the thesis that if the father is not the head of the family, there can be nothing but chaos. He says that the father is responsible for structure and form and for establishing the family standards, character, direction, and strength. And if he doesn't do that, it castrates the family.

We know that fathers are being attacked. They're being attacked when they're diverted from their wives and children to fulfill their own desires, to be the macho man, and to be self-satisfied. They lose their concentration on loving the family, providing for the family, caring for the family, and offering them strength, stability, character, leadership, and solid teaching—bringing them up in the things of God. Now, apart from Christ, we know that those things are impossible. But it's sad to see that so many Christian fathers have become preoccupied with the television set, their businesses, making money, accumulating material things, lusting after other women, and other things that tend to overthrow their priorities.

2. Mothers attacked

Mothers are being forced out of the home. By 1990, perhaps 45 percent of the United States' work force will be women. Already 6 million children under the age of six have working mothers. Nearly half of all children under the age of eighteen have working mothers. Women are intimidated into leaving the home. They're told, "Don't let yourself settle for being a homemaker. You're too good for that. Push yourself out into the world." They become exposed to the temptations of other men, material things, worldly philosophies, and worldly lifestyles. I believe this failure of mothers is a result of the failure of fathers to give spiritual strength and character to their families.

3. Children attacked

  a) Abandoned at home

According to David Elkind in an article in *Psychology Today*, "One major change is the form of middle-class mothering. For a mother to work voluntarily while her children were young was once seen as a sign of bad parenting, a rejection of the maternal role. But today, going to work and placing a child with a care-taker or in a day-care center [or at a preschool] is accepted practice. For many children, that means coming home to empty houses after school and tending to their own meals, clothing, hygiene" ("Growing Up Faster" [Feb. 1979]: 41). And, as one woman added, it also includes locking doors on school holidays and having the children sit in front of the TV.

  b) Influenced by TV

    (1) Violent role models

Dr. Walter Menninger, a psychiatrist connected with Topeka State Hospital, said we are raising a generation of violently aggressive women who are being formed through children's exposure to TV's fantasy female super-heroes ("Effects of TV Aggression on Girls Worry Expert," *Los Angeles Times*, 22 Feb. 1979). Some TV shows are shoving girls outside a normal understanding and comprehension of God's role for women.

    (2) Godless morality

      (*a*) According to Ben Stein in *The View from Sunset Boulevard*, interviews with the forces behind television (executives, producers, writers) reveal that they are systematically attempting to overthrow traditional American values (New York: Basic Books, 1979). That is accomplished primarily through the situation comedy: you can get people to buy a whole new philosophy if you can get them to laugh with it.

(b) TV characters consume ten times more alcohol than coffee.

(c) According to the National Federation of Decency (Fall 1978), 88 percent of all sex depicted on TV is outside marriage.

(3) Stifled communication

In many cases, parents don't talk to their children because they're too busy watching TV.

c) Raised by day-care centers

The Denver Post ran an article about a group of day-care workers who were trying to start a union to protect themselves from abusive children (Marice Doll, "Day-Care Mothers Air Gripes, 'Pain,'" 5 Feb. 1979). The article said children arrived "with runny noses, chicken pox, and bad manners." The day-care workers had to teach potty training, table manners, respect, and just about everything else—all at about a fifty-to-one ratio. These day-care workers were so frustrated they hoped to form a union to get some help.

d) Abused according to statistics

(1) An estimated 750,000 children live in foster homes, residential facilities, institutions, mental hospitals, or are in prisons (Curtis J. Sitomer, "Who Speaks for the Child? The Right to a Home and Family," *The Christian Science Monitor*, 6 Feb. 1979).

(2) Four out of ten children will live in a broken home.

(3) Eighteen million children are currently living with step-parents.

(4) Between seven and fourteen million children will become alcoholics, based on the statistics con-

cerning children of alcoholics who become alcoholics themselves.

(5) Sixty-five out of every one thousand children between the ages of seven and eleven have received psychiatric help.

(6) American children are indulged with more than 4 billion dollars of toys each year—more than the gross national product of sixty-three nations.

(7) The average age of beginning smokers has dropped from fourteen to ten.

(8) One million young girls between the ages of twelve and seventeen get pregnant every year.

(9) Ten million minors have venereal disease, and five thousand new victims contract it every day.

(10) One child in five uses drugs twice a week.

(11) The only age group with increased births in America is girls from age eleven to fourteen.

Our children are being attacked by an anti-God philosophy. We can't stand around in indifference and expect them to turn out all right in the end. Fighting against this encroaching evil system is a full-time job.

C. The Specifics of the Attack on the Family

1. The curse of sin

The curse of sin is built into the family. The curse causes men to be oppressive, despotic, and chauvinistic; it causes women to want to rule over men and usurp their position of authority, and it causes children to rebel. It is only in a family where its members are Spirit-filled and obedient to the Word of God that God's standards for the family can be fulfilled.

Children Committing Suicide?

The suicide rate among children is staggering. Between 10 and 15 percent of children have tried or have contemplated suicide. Charlotte Ross, director of the San Mateo Suicide Prevention Center, said children as young as six or seven are trying to kill themselves ("Suicides Among Young Persons Said to Have Tripled in 20 Years," *The New York Times*, 11 Feb. 1979). And she laid the blame on what she calls "the way our society has of alienating kids."

Lois Timnick, human behavior writer for the *Los Angeles Times*, wrote an article about child suicide ("They're Sad, Young and Want to Die," 25 July 1978). She says, "For years the experts questioned whether young children could really suffer severe depression and intentionally seek death. Now it seems clear that they do both, and that many 'accidents'—like swallowing poison or darting into heavy traffic—are in fact conscious or unconscious suicide attempts."

Timnick quotes one authority as saying, "For the younger aged children, the most frequent immediate event leading to referral [clinical treatment] was perceived or imagined abandonment by a parent figure." In other words, when a child feels he has been abandoned by his parent, whether imagined or real, it is the first step in the direction of suicide. According to this article, violence between a mother and father, the birth of a new brother or sister, competition for the parents' love, and a mother's decision to go back to work can all be interpreted by children as rejection and can contribute to attempts of suicide.

2. The failure of parents

   Parents have failed—even Christian parents have failed. God can restore us, forgive us, and help us get our families back together again. We need to understand the reality of what God is asking. The emotional and spiritual needs of children are not being met. We are allowing the world to raise our children by allowing them to sit in front of the TV and watch the filth the world pumps out.

   Your children depend on you; you can't hire someone to do what you aren't willing to do. As one woman said, "You will never get children to respond to what people

99

do for money but you won't do for love." If you are gone all the time—whether it's because of work or other activities—and if you don't talk to your children, you're going to lose them. The sad fact is, what starts out in your life as a great joy can end up as the biggest heartbreak.

The Fallacy of the Financial Need for the Wife to Work

In most families the wife probably doesn't need to work. Why? Because in most cases the family doesn't really need the money. Recently on Chicago network television, one of the leading financial experts in our country was talking about this problem. Amazingly, he said that indulgent materialism is what has forced the woman into the work force. He said that often by the time a couple pays the increased income tax and supports the wife's wardrobe, transportation, meals outside the home, and child care, the actual increase in income could not exceed 10 percent. He also said that because the indebtedness of the family is usually increased, even that gain may be ultimately lost in the payment of additional interest on debts. He stated that the families in the U.S. carrying the largest unpaid debt are the families with both husband and wife working.

We're spending so much time acquiring things that we're forgetting our children. Children are treasures that God has given to us to care for and to be raised—not to be like us—but to be like Jesus Christ.

Are Children Getting Older at a Younger Age?

Do you realize that the age of puberty is now two to five years earlier than it was in the past? In the eighteenth century, the Bach choirboys who sang soprano had to leave the choir when they were eighteen years old because their voices began to change. Now adolescence begins at an average of thirteen years of age. The age of puberty is getting lower and lower. In fact, according to Anne C. Petersen in an article in *Psychology Today*, it lowers four months per decade ("Can Puberty Come Any Earlier?" [Feb. 1979]: 45). In 1900, human growth continued to an average age of twenty-six. Today growth stops, on an average, between seventeen and eighteen years of age. In 1600, the average age of puberty varied between seventeen and twenty. In 1900 it was more than fourteen.

Children are becoming more aware of their physical and sexual world at an earlier age. People may think children in junior high don't have problems in the sexual area, but they do, and they desperately need adults not only to guide them but to police their activities. School principals have told me that even sixth graders can have major problems in the area of sexual discovery.

This lowering age of puberty has many causes. One factor is early exposure to sex. Sex is pounded into children's brains when they turn on the TV and when they walk by a magazine rack; it's there constantly—sexual music, books, magazines, television, and movies. Children are shoved into a sex-mad thinking pattern before their minds are able to handle it. Their bodies are running ahead of their minds, and few receive the parental instruction they need. And you can't just teach them, you have to police them, because they don't have the ability to maintain proper standards yet.

Another factor comes with what David Elkind in an article in *Psychology Today* calls "hurried children" ("Growing Up Faster" [Feb. 1979]: 40). Young girls are wearing makeup and dressing like older women. Young boys are wearing clothes styled after men's clothing. There are few distinctions. Children are shoved into an overachievement world. Parents push their children into gifted classes before they're ready. They are pushed into adult life-styles long before they're given the proper instructions on how to handle them.

3. The emergence of humanistic philosophy

F. M. Esfandiary, quoted in an article in the *Los Angeles Times,* said that he looks for a world where there will be no schools, no families, and no parent-child relationships ("Utopia Without Families," 20 Mar. 1978). To free the child, he says, we must do away with parenthood—marriage must go. We must settle for nothing less than the total elimination of the family. That philosophy is being propagated by many humanists—and their arguments are effective.

a) The International Year of the Child

On April 4, 1978, President Carter issued an executive order proclaiming 1979 as the International Year of the Child (IYC) in the United States. It recognized the twentieth anniversary of the "Child's Bill of Rights," which was established by the United Nations Educational, Scientific, and Cultural Organization (UNESCO) in 1959. Many people's initial reaction was, "Great, children need help." The philosophy behind that idea, however, was as satanic as everything else attacking the home.

(1) Its source

The IYC was inseparably linked to the International Women's Year (IWY) and to the International Women's Decade (IWD). The years from 1976 to 1985 were designated as the decade of the woman. Betty Friedan, a prime intellectual mover in the woman's liberation movement, commented on a conversation she had at the World Conference for Women in Mexico City: "I had a curious luncheon invitation from a woman involved with [an] old-time Communist Woman's group. . . . [They said] did I know, by the way, it was they who introduced the resolution to make 1975 International Women's Year?" (*It Changed My Life* [New York: Random, 1976], p. 345). So the whole concept was atheistic, socialistic, and humanistic at its roots.

(2) Its efforts

The IYC, IWY, and the IWD are all efforts towards socialism. One ultimate end of socialism is to take children out of the home and family and educate them by the state. Why? Because if parents don't have their children, they can't pass on any righteous standards, moral values, ethics, religion, or political feelings. Parents can't pass on anything if they don't have their children. (In the U.S. Congress, there are bills that have been on the floor since 1971 that recommend taking children out of the home at the age of six months, putting them into government day-care centers, educating them by the government until they reach six years of age, and then putting them in public schools.) That's a socialistic, atheistic, godless approach to destroying the family.

b) The Child's Bill of Rights

The "Declaration of the Rights of the Child" that the United Nations put out in 1959 seemed innocuous. But when you see how it's being defined today, it's a different story. From their own writings, we discover how international social planners are trying to "liberate" children.

(1) Liberation from traditional moral values

"The real solution requires a fundamental change in the value commitment and the actions of the persons who control the public and private sectors of our common life [such as] parents" (*White House Conference on Children, Report to the President*, 1970, p. 66).

"Day-care is a powerful institution. . . . A day-care program that ministers to a child from six months to six years of age has over 8,000 hours to teach him values, fears, beliefs and behaviors" (*White House Conference on Children*, p. 278). You can believe that those values, fears, beliefs, and behaviors will not be God's. Gloria Steinem said, "By the year 2000 we will, I hope, raise our children to believe in human potential, not God" ("How Will We Raise Our Children in the Year 2000?" *Saturday Review of Education* [March 1973]: 30).

(2) Liberation from parental authority

Some officials have said, "We recommend that laws dealing with the rights of parents be reexamined and changed when they infringe on the rights of children" (*White House Conference on Chil-*

103

dren, p. 361). One of the things experts talk about is physical punishment. Some day you may not be able to spank or discipline your child. Humanist psychologist Richard Farson says we have to free children from physical punishment, we have to free them to vote, and we have to give them total sexual freedom (*Birthrights* [New York: Macmillan, 1974]). Such people want to have a classless, sexless, Godless, Christless society.

(3) Liberation from discrimination

"The child shall be protected from practices which may foster racial, religious and any other form of discrimination" (Principle 10, 1959 United Nation's Declaration of the Rights of the Child). That "protection" has been interpreted to forbid Buddhist parents to teach their children Buddhism and Christian parents to teach their children Christianity. Children would be removed from homes so that their parents would have no influence on them at all. They would be "protected" from their parents' religion.

(4) Liberation from nationalism and patriotism

A book prepared by UNESCO says that "as long as the child breathes the poisoned air of nationalism, education in world-mindedness can produce only rather precarious results. As we have pointed out, it is frequently the family that infects the child with extreme nationalism. The school should therefore use the means described earlier to combat family attitudes that favour [that]" (*Towards World Understanding*, book 5, 1953, p. 58). In other words, they propose preventing your child from loving his country. They say we need to cut children loose from past political traditions, morals, values, and religion.

As we try to raise godly children, we are fighting a powerful enemy. The enemy has captured the media, and that media is in the TV, in books, in papers, in music, in schools

—everywhere. And unless you commit yourself to raising your children, it's going to be difficult.

It's getting tougher and tougher to live as a Christian in this world. It's not easy. Commit yourselves to your children, or you'll wake up one day with tragedy on your hands. I thank God for His Word, because it tells how to counter this movement that threatens to engulf our societies and destroy our families. Everything is in the Word of God. You may ask, "What could a two-thousand-year-old book have to say about this?" The Bible may have been written two thousand years ago, but it's alive today because times haven't changed, men haven't changed, and certainly God hasn't changed. What He says today is absolutely as current, up to date, and essential for us.

Lesson

I. THE SUBMISSION OF THE CHILD (vv. 1-3)

"Children, obey your parents in the Lord; for this is right. Honor thy father and mother (which is the first commandment with promise), that it may be well with thee, and thou mayest live long on the earth."

This is the only command in the Bible given specifically to children. The word *children* used in verse 1 is *ta tekna* in the Greek text. It doesn't mean "little babies"; it refers to any offspring under parental control. So anyone at any age living in the house who identifies himself as a child of that family is to obey his parents (an action) and honor his father and mother (an attitude).

II. THE SUBMISSION OF THE PARENTS (v. 4)

"And, ye fathers [lit., "parents"], provoke not your children to wrath, but bring them up in the nurture and admonition of the Lord."

That's a tough job. Bring your children up in the nurture and admonition of the Lord; don't leave it to the world to raise them. If you do, the world will raise them, but when they get done, it will be a tragedy.

Parents, you'd better take your stand with Jesus Christ, make a conscious break with the ungodly system of the world, and commit yourselves to your family. Also, realize that no matter what mistakes you've made in the past, God graciously forgives. And remember the promise in Proverbs 22:6, "Train up a child in the way he should go and, when he is old, he will not depart from it." You do your job and bring your child up in the way that God wants him brought up, and God will honor that.

Focusing on the Facts

1. What statistic indicates that we have moved a long way from the divine plan for the family (see p. 92)?
2. In what sense was the nation of Israel a means to an end (see pp. 92-93)?
3. How was God's truth passed on to a new generation in ancient Israel (see pp. 93-94)?
4. What has been Satan's plan against the family? Why (see pp. 94-95)?
5. What results in a family if the father is not its head? What is the father responsible for in a family (see p. 95)?
6. How are mothers being attacked (see pp. 95-96)?
7. What is the cause for the failure of many women to be dedicated mothers (see pp. 95-96)?
8. How have children often been abandoned? What often influences them more than their parents do? Explain its negative effects (see pp. 96-97).
9. Why would a day-care center probably not give the same quality of attention that a mother might give her child (see p. 97)?
10. How does the curse of sin effect children? What does it cause them to do (see pp. 98-99)?
11. Describe the reasons children have for committing suicide (see p. 99).
12. What has forced many women into the work force? What American families have carried the largest unpaid debt (see p. 100)?
13. How does early exposure to sexual situations challenge today's children (see pp. 100-101)?

14. What is the ultimate end of socialism regarding children? What will that prevent parents from doing (see pp. 102-3)?
15. From what are social planners trying to liberate children (pp. 103-5)?
16. What is the only command in the Bible ever given specifically to children (see p. 105)?
17. According to Ephesians 6:4, how are parents supposed to raise their children (see p. 105)?

Pondering the Principles

1. How would you rate the quality of communication between you and your children? Does your job demand so much time that they sometimes seem like strangers? When you get home, do you find yourself distracted by tiredness, television, or household duties? Think of some creative ways you could make maximum use of the time you have available for them. Maybe you could wash the car or run errands together. Maybe you could meet for lunch at a park in the middle of the week. Plan some family outings for the next few months, being careful that other things don't cause you to cancel those family times, which are extremely important to children. If they feel your time with them is a low priority, they will doubt the genuineness of your love for them.

2. Realizing that Christians are fighting a powerful enemy, we must take extreme care in how we raise our children. Public education for the most part is humanistic. Television offers little that is of value, and much that contradicts godly values. The friends our children play with may come from homes with no spiritual training. Don't allow the world to be the sole influence in raising your children. What things are you doing—besides sending your children off to Sunday school—to instill godly standards in them? Do they know how God desires them to respond? Use every chance you can to help them evaluate situations from a biblical viewpoint and encourage them to respond accordingly.

7
The Divine Pattern for the Family—Part 2
The Role of the Child

Outline

Introduction

Lesson
I. The Submission of the Child (vv. 1-3)
   A. The Act of Obedience (v. 1)
      1. "Children"
      2. "Obey your parents"
        a) The definition
        b) The design
        c) The disaster
      3. "In the Lord"
        a) The sphere
        b) The specifics
      4. "For this is right"
        a) The reason
        b) The references
   B. The Attitude of Honor (vv. 2-3)
      1. The precept (v. 2*a*)
        a) To honor with reverence and respect
        b) To honor with financial support
      2. The primacy (v. 2*b*)
      3. The promise (v. 3)
        a) Quality of life
        b) Quantity of life

Introduction

James Dobson tells a story about a frog who was put into a shallow pan of cool water. Slowly the water was heated. Almost imperceptibly, the temperature began to rise, gradually moving to the boiling point. The frog continued, however, to sit in the pan, totally unaware of the rising temperature—even when the steam began to curl. Eventually he was boiled to death, although at any point he could have jumped out and avoided that fate (*Dare to Discipline* [Wheaton, Ill.: Tyndale, 1970], p. 15).

I think that is an apt illustration of what has happened, in many cases, to the American family. We have been sitting in what appeared, at first, to be rather cool water: a God-fearing country where the environment was in many ways conducive to spirituality. However, while we have been content to sit in the midst of the system, it has gradually been heating up and drifting far from where we first felt secure. The family is being destroyed, and Christian families should have jumped out of the pan a long time ago. When you consider that only 7 percent of Americans currently live in what is known as a traditional family, where the father is the breadwinner and the mother is the homemaker, you know we've been complacent far too long. When you stop to realize that the divorce rate among Christians is almost as high as it is among non-Christians, you know we've been apathetic. It's high time that we escape the evil world system that is engulfing us and begin to establish ourselves on the basis of God's revelation. We can no longer count on the luxury of living in a Christian country that is conducive to our spiritual well-being. That is just not the case. Satan has hit the family with an all-out attack, and we need to reawaken ourselves to the biblical priorities if we're going to get out of the pan before it's too late.

The principles we're going to study, which are related to the interpersonal relationships in the family, are possible only where there is an acknowledgment of the lordship of Jesus Christ. Apart from Him, these principles become only nice ideas that are impossible to fulfill. But when an individual gives his life to Christ, when Christ moves into a family, and when that family is filled with the Spirit of God, it then becomes possible—even reasonable and normal—to function according to those principles.

110

As we look at a Christ-centered, Spirit-filled family, what are the factors involved? First of all, the submission of the child (vv. 1-3) and then the submission of the parents, who are submitting to a God-ordained standard (v. 4).

Lesson

I. THE SUBMISSION OF THE CHILD (vv. 1-3)

A. The Act of Obedience (v. 1)

"Children, obey your parents in the Lord; for this is right."

1. "Children"

The word for "children" (Gk., *tekna*) is not used to speak of an infant. It is a broad term used to speak of all off-spring (i.e., anyone born from another person). We are all children in the strictest sense of this word. But the idea here is that anyone who is still under the roof of, under the domination of, under the control of, or under the responsibility of his parents is to obey them. I believe obedience to your parents, which begins when you are in the home, will in a sense extend through the rest of your life. You will still have a deep sensitivity to respond to what your parents say, no matter how old you are, if you've learned that from your earliest years. But as long as you're under their care, and they accept the responsibility to care for you, you must obey them.

2. "Obey your parents"

a) The definition

The word *obey* is a simple yet graphic term in the Greek. It is the compound word *hupakouō*, which is from *akouō*, meaning "to hear," and the preposition *hup*, meaning "under." So the Holy Spirit is saying, "Children, get under the authority of your parents and listen." The society we live in is saying that we need to liberate children from parental authority. They are saying that a child must have the right to his

111

own destiny, his own religion, his own thoughts, and his own perspective on economics and morality. But the Bible says the contrary. Children have no business being liberated; they are to get under the authority of their parents and listen to what parents say. That is God's basic design and always has been.

The Key to Right Relationships

God first introduces His law in Exodus 20. In examining the Ten Commandments, we find they are divided into two parts: the first four commandments deal with man's relationship to God, and the last six deal with man's relationship to man. In moving from the commands regarding human relationships, verse 12 says, "Honor thy father and thy mother, that thy days may be long upon the land which the Lord thy God giveth thee." Notice that this is the only statement in the Ten Commandments on the way the family is to function. Why? Because it is sufficient to produce right relationships within the home and society. In fact, it is the key to all relationships, because a person who grows up with a sense of obedience, discipline, reverence, awe, and respect for his parents will be someone who can make any other kind of human relationship work.

God was serious about a child's respect and obedience to his parents. Exodus 21:15 says, "He that smiteth his father, or his mother, shall be surely put to death." Verse 17 says, "He that curseth his father, or his mother, shall surely be put to death." All human relationships are based on what is learned in childhood. If you learn reverence, awe, respect, and obedience as a child, then the basis for having proper relationships will be present throughout your life. Undisciplined children who did not know how to respect authority or to honor their parents would have created a chaotic world, so God said to the Jews that the life of a rebellious child was to be taken away.

b) The design

God's basic design for children is that they be obedient to their parents. If you're still living at home, whether you're in elementary school, junior high school, high school, or college, you have the responsibility to obey your parents. But on the other hand, it is the parents' responsibility to teach their children to be obedient. Why? Frankly, because children are not that way normally. You don't have to teach children to disobey; they know how to do that. The first thing you have to teach them is how to obey. Children come into the world disobedient because they have inherited a sin nature, and the only way they'll learn obedience is to be taught. So it's the design of God for children to be obedient to their parents' instruction, but parents must also give instruction that their children can obey. That is well illustrated throughout the book of Proverbs.

(1) "My son, hear the instruction of thy father, and forsake not the law of thy mother" (1:8). That is the keynote of the book. Children are to listen to what their parents say, not because they are infallible, but because it is necessary that children learn authority and submission, and that they learn to be disciplined.

(2) "My son, if thou wilt receive my words, and lay up my commandments with thee" (2:1).

(3) "My son, forget not my law, but let thine heart keep my commandments" (3:1).

(4) "Hear, ye children, the instruction of a father, and attend to know understanding; for I give you good doctrine; forsake ye not my law. For I was my father's son, tender and only beloved in the sight of my mother. He taught me also, and said unto me, Let thine heart retain my words; keep my commandments, and live" (4:1-4). That is how God wants truth to be passed on: from one generation to the next. A child must be commanded, and he must be made to listen and obey. Since his natural proclivity is toward sinfulness, if you spare him teaching and discipline, you will spoil him.

(5) "Hear, O my son, and receive my sayings, and the years of thy life shall be many" (4:10).

113

(6) "My son, attend unto my wisdom, and bow thine ear to my understanding, that thou mayest regard discretion, and that thy lips may keep knowledge" (5:1-2).

(7) "My son, keep my words, and lay up my commandments with thee. Keep my commandments, and live, and my law as the apple of thine eye" (7:1-2). As carefully as you protect the pupil of your eye, so too the law of God, given by your parents, is to be protected.

(8) "Hearken unto me now, therefore, O ye children, and attend to the words of my mouth" (7:24).

(9) "Now, therefore, hearken unto me, O ye children; for blessed are they who keep my ways. Hear instruction, and be wise, and refuse it not" (8:32-33).

(10) "Whoso loveth instruction loveth knowledge, but he that hateth reproof is stupid" (12:1). Why? Because he'll grow up undisciplined.

(11) "A wise son heareth his father's instruction" (13:1).

(12) "A fool despiseth his father's instruction" (15:5).

The point is obvious. The Bible says children are to obey.

Why Must Children Be Closely Guided and Made to Obey?

Children have a basic problem: they are children, and as such, are lacking in four areas. Those areas are delineated in Luke 2:52. In this verse we see Jesus Christ, from the perspective of His humanity, as a twelve-year-old child. He was all that a child could be—apart from being sinful. According to Luke 2:52, from the time He was twelve until His ministry, He "increased in wisdom and stature, and in favor with God and man." Thus, the four areas in which children lack are: wisdom (mental needs), stature (physical needs), favor with man (social needs), and favor with God (spiritual needs).

1. Children lack wisdom

   Children lack discretion, instruction, and knowledge. When a baby comes into the world, his brain is void of information. So whatever he's going to know must first be taught to him. Also, children have no discretion; they don't know what's right and what's wrong. They don't know the right foods to eat, and they don't know not to put certain things in their mouths. Those things must be taught.

2. Children lack stature

   Children are weak physically; they are unable to support or sustain themselves. Parents have the responsibility of feeding them, nourishing them, and making sure they get the proper rest. Children can't fend for themselves; they can't make it in the world alone, so the parents must protect them.

3. Children lack favor with men

   Children are not socially acclimated. The dominant trait of a newborn child is selfishness. He can't conceive of anything but "I want it now" or "It's mine." It's difficult to teach children to share. They don't know any of the social graces like humility or unselfishness; they must be taught.

4. Children lack favor with God

   In the spiritual area, children don't naturally grow to love God. When they are little, they will comprehend God, but without proper instruction they will drift away. Proverbs 22:6 says, "Train up a child in the way he should go and, when he is old, he will not depart from it." That is the responsibility of the parents.

   c) The disaster

      Children face problems in the mental, physical, social, and spiritual areas of life. Parents, you must provide an environment in which your children can grow in those areas of inadequacy. If you don't provide for spiritual, social, physical, and mental growth in all the dimensions of life, you're going to come up with "a generation that curseth their father, and doth not bless their mother. . . . That are pure in their own eyes, and yet are not washed from their filthiness" (Prov. 30:11-12). In other words, you're going to have an evil, unruly generation. And, according to verse 17, when you get that kind of a generation, "The eye that mocketh at his father, and despiseth to obey his mother, the ravens of the valley shall pick it out, and the young eagles shall eat it." That is God's judgment.

Look around you. We have raised a generation of young people who do only what's right in their own eyes. They mock their fathers, despise their mothers, and are unruly. Children need to be taught to obey. How? By discipline and by example.

3. "In the Lord"

   a) The sphere

   When Paul says children are to obey their parents "in the Lord," he's saying that obedience is in the sphere of serving, pleasing, honoring, and worshiping the Lord for His glory.

   b) The specifics

   Colossians 3:20 says, "Children, obey your parents in all things." Does that mean children are to obey their parents even if they tell them to do evil? No. That's where they have to stop. In Acts 5:29 Peter and John say, "We ought to obey God rather than men." When God's commands intersect with men's commands, you must obey God. Daniel was told not to pray, but he prayed anyway (Dan. 6:10). Some parents have told their children not to worship Christ, read the Bible, pray, fellowship with other believers, or share their testimony. But the Bible says to do those things. So children are to obey their parents in everything, except when it goes against God's stated revelation. Then they have to be willing to suffer the consequences of violating their parents' desires (cf. Matt. 10:37-39; Luke 14:25-27).

4. "For this is right"

   a) The reason

   Why are children to obey their parents? Because verse 1 says, "For this is right." You may ask, "But where's the psychological evidence? Who did the case studies? Where's the philosopher's opinion here?" You don't need any other evidence except what is right here. God says it's right.

   The word translated "right" is the Greek word *dikaios*, which means "righteous," "just," or "right." It's used of God, Christ, the Word, holy living, and obeying one's parents, all of which are right and good.

   b) The references

   The word *right* and its corollary are used 183 times in the New Testament alone. God has established what is right. Some examples of its use in both Old and New Testaments are in Nehemiah 9:13; Psalm 19:8; 119:75, 128; Hosea 14:9; Romans 7:12; 12:2; and Revelation 15:3; 16:5, 7; 19:2.

B. The Attitude of Honor (vv. 2-3)

   "Honor thy father and mother (which is the first commandment with promise), that it may be well with thee, and thou mayest live long on the earth."

   Honor is the attitude behind the act. The act is obedience, and honor is the attitude. Remember that an act without the proper attitude is hypocrisy. If you do what your parents tell you to do but you hate it and you're unwilling and nasty about it, then you're a hypocrite. If you do what your parents tell you to do but you're bitter, fearful, reluctant, and selfish, that's not the right spirit. God is after the attitude much more than He's after the act, because if the attitude is right, the act will follow. But a right act with a wrong attitude is nothing but hypocrisy.

1. The precept (v. 2*a*)

"Honor thy father and mother"

a) To honor with reverence and respect

The word translated "honor" is the Greek word *ti-maō*, which simply means "to reverence, to worship, to hold in awe, to value at a high price." It is used to speak of Jesus and God the Father in John 5:23. We are to have this attitude of honor, respect, and reverence toward our parents all our lives.

b) To honor with financial support

Honoring our parents is not an attitude only. In Matthew 15:1-6, Jesus interprets the commandment "Honor thy father and mother" as referring to financial support. He uses the word *honor* the way it's used in 1 Timothy 5:17. It can be translated "to give money to" or "to pay."

So, the Old Testament law of honoring one's parents meant that as long as a person lived, he was to respect and support his parents. During the first half of a person's life, the parents give everything they have to supply the needs of their children. When they get to the point in life where they're no longer able to meet their own needs, it becomes the responsibility of their children to take care of them. That is God's way of making families stick together. The parents raise the children, and when the children are grown, they take care of their parents while also raising their own children, who are going to take care of them while they are raising their children. That way the family always stays together, and the righteous seed keeps being passed along.

2. The primacy (v. 2*b*)

"Which is the first commandment with promise."

The first four commandments of the Decalogue were related to God and didn't have a promise with them. You may ask, "Why is the fifth commandment so important that God puts a promise with it?" Because it's the key to all human relationships and the passing on of a righteous heritage.

3. The promise (v. 3)

"That it may be well with thee, and that thou mayest live long on the earth."

a) Quality of life

"That it may be well with thee" refers to a full, rich life.

b) Quantity of life

"That thou mayest live long on the earth" refers to a long life—living out the fullness of the time God has allotted to you.

When we are obedient children, when we honor our parents, and when our relationships in the home are right, we'll have a full and rich lifetime here, we'll live with Him in the kingdom for a thousand years, and we'll live with Him in the new heavens and the new earth for eternity.

Focusing on the Facts

1. How can the American family be likened to a frog in a pan of water that is gradually heated to boiling (see p. 110)?
2. To whom specifically is Paul's command in Ephesians 6:1 directed (see p. 111)?
3. What does society advise us to do with children? What does the Bible say (see pp. 111-12)?
4. Why is the command to honor one's parents the key to all other relationships in society (see p. 112)?
5. What was the consequence of a child's rebelling against his parents in Israel (see p. 112)?

6. Why do parents have a responsibility to teach their children to be obedient (see p. 113)?
7. In what four areas are children lacking? Explain each (pp. 114-15).
8. What are the results of not providing the proper environment for your children's growth (Prov. 30:11-12, 17; see p. 116)?
9. What does it mean to obey one's parents "in the Lord" (Eph. 6:1; see pp. 116-17)?
10. Should a child ever draw a line in obeying his parents? Explain (see pp. 116-17).
11. What must a child be willing to face when choosing God's Word over his parent's desires (Luke 14:25-27; see p. 117)?
12. What should be the attitude behind the act of obedience? What is an act without the proper attitude (see pp. 117-18)?
13. What attitude are we to have toward our parents all our lives? What else should we be willing to do for them (see pp. 118-19)?
14. Why is keeping the fifth commandment rewarded with a promise? What is the nature of that promise (see p. 119)?

Pondering the Principles

1. Parents, how are you helping your children increase "in wisdom and stature, and in favor with God and man" (Luke 2:52)? Are you holding your breath and closing your eyes, hoping that your children will automatically turn out all right? Your children are like an investment that must be constantly tended for maximum yield. Unless you know how to read the trends in the economy, adjusting your investment accordingly, there is a good chance you could end up with a loss. Similarly, you need to carefully oversee the valuable investment of your children. Make sure it can weather the depressions and recessions of growing up in a ever-changing society. How are you helping them discern right from wrong? Think of some ways you can help them grow in social and spiritual maturity. Do you know of neighborhood children who are being neglected by their parents? Encourage them to interact with your family so you might introduce a godly influence into their lives.

2. Do you honor your parents as God asks us to, even if they are not Christians? The manner in which you treat your parents will set an example for the way your children will treat you. Do you criticize or ridicule them when you talk to others about them?

Are you unwilling to forgive a wrong they may have committed against you? Do you graciously tolerate their criticism of you? If the family you grew up in lacked a healthy family atmosphere, there is still time to change that. Determine what you need to do to resolve any differences or meet any needs they have. Do they need financial assistance? Can they benefit from your spiritual guidance? Do they have any errands you can run or chores you can do for them? If they live far away from you, communicate with them by letter or phone on a regular basis. Make the last years they spend on this earth their most rewarding.

8
The Divine Pattern for the Family—Part 3
The Role of the Parents

Outline

Introduction
A. The Call of God to Be Separate from the World
   1. As seen in Ephesians
   2. As seen in Leviticus
B. The Consequences of Being Victimized by the World
C. The Corruption of God's Design for Children
   1. The world's view
   2. God's intention
D. The Cause of the Present Chaos in Rearing Children
   1. As seen by the Houston police department
   2. As seen by a Christian psychiatrist
   3. As seen by the Minnesota Crime Commission

Review
 I. The Submission of the Child (vv. 1-3)

Lesson
 II. The Submission of the Parents (v. 4)
    A. The Parents Identified
    B. The Parents Instructed
       1. The negative
       2. The positive
          a) "Nurture"
          b) "Admonition"

Introduction

A. The Call of God to Be Separate from the World

1. As seen in Ephesians

God is calling on us to be different from the world. We're to have different marriages, different families, and different life-styles. In Ephesians, Paul says we're not to walk as the heathen walk (4:17). We're to walk in love (5:2), not in lust; in light (5:8), not in darkness; in wisdom (5:15), not in foolishness; in the Spirit (5:18), not in the flesh. We're not to be selfish—each man for himself; we're to be unselfish—each for the other. We're not to be possessed by our own ego; we're to be controlled by the Spirit of God. We're to be different.

2. As seen in Leviticus

From the beginning when God called out the nation of Israel to be His people, it was clear that they were to be separate from the world. In Leviticus 18, when God lays down the law of behavior for Israel, this is what He says regarding the difference between His people and the world: "After the doings of the land of Egypt, wherein ye dwelt, shall ye not do; and after the doings of the land of Canaan, to which I bring you, shall ye not do; neither shall ye walk in their ordinances. Ye shall do mine ordinances, and keep my statutes, to walk therein: I am the Lord your God. Ye shall therefore keep my statutes, and mine ordinances, which if a man do, he shall live in them: I am the Lord" (vv. 3-5).

Later on in the same chapter the Lord says, "Defile not ye yourselves in any of these things; for in all these the nations are defiled, which I cast out before you. And the land is defiled; therefore I do visit the iniquity thereof upon it, and the land itself vomiteth out her inhabitants" (vv. 24-25). In other words, He says, "Why would you do that for which other nations were judged?" He continues in verse 26: "Ye shall therefore keep my statutes and mine ordinances, and shall not commit any of these abominations; neither any of your own nation, nor any stranger that sojourneth among you." And verse 30 repeats the same thought: "Therefore shall ye keep mine ordinance, that ye commit not any of these abominable customs, which were committed before you, and that ye defile not yourselves therein: I am the Lord your God."

From the beginning, it was God's intention that His people be separate, set apart, and not conformed to the world. Yet that's extremely difficult. And when we come to the area of marriage and family, it's obvious that we have become victimized by the system. Our desire to be what our society tells us to be has caused the destruction of marriage and the family in many ways. Yet God is still giving us the same message in Ephesians 6 as He did in Leviticus 18: "Do it My way. Don't listen to what the world says. You're not of the world anymore, you have overcome the world, you are out of the world. Do things My way; follow my standards."

B. The Consequences of Being Victimized by the World

Unless we understand God's standards for the family and begin to put them in operation in your own homes, we will have nothing to pass on to the next generation. You may say, "That will never happen in America." Really? Did you know that Russia was once a Christian nation? In fact, Russia was in many ways the heart of Eastern Orthodox Christianity. Eastern Europe was once a Christian area where the Eastern church reigned supreme. And there was even a time in China, during the great days of Hudson Taylor, when the church was being founded and there was great Christian growth. Yet now in all those areas, generation after generation has been raised without any concept of God or Christianity.

There's a Chinese proverb that says, "One generation plants the trees, and the next gets the shade." I don't know whether there is much "tree-planting" going on for the shade of the next generation. How are we planning to shelter our children from the heat of the world's evil sun? What are we doing to protect them against those disintegrating rays? I'm concerned that we not just sit by idly and think that our children and the next generation are going to turn out all right on their own—because they're not. Until we come out of the world and begin to stand apart, and until we begin to define the biblical life-style and teach it to our children—passing it on, no matter what it costs—we're not going to have anything for the next generation.

C. The Corruption of God's Design for Children

1. The world's view

   Much of the world today doesn't even want children. Consider the following:

   a) One-third of all married couples who are of child-bearing age are permanently sterilized. They don't want children.

   b) One survey done in America showed that 70 percent of the parents surveyed would not have children if they had to do it over again (Lance Morrow, "Wondering If Children Are Necessary," *Time* [5 Mar. 1979]:42).

   c) There is an organization in America called N.O.N. (The National Organization of Non-Parents). They say they don't want to complicate their lives with children.

   What are we doing with the future generation? Even when they are born, it seems as though they are left to themselves.

2. God's intention

   I can't understand how people could not want to have children. Scripture is abundantly clear that God gives children; they are a gift from the Lord.

   a) God is the source of children (Gen. 4:1, 25; 16:10; 17:16, 20; 29:31-35; 30:2, 6, 17-20; 33:5, 48:9; Ruth 4:13; 1 Sam. 1:19-20).

   b) Children are a heritage and a reward from the Lord (Ps. 127:3).

c) Children are a source of joy (Ps. 113:9; 127:4-5; Prov. 23:24).

God gives children. He gives them as a blessing, as a benediction, and as a grace to life. And the more children you have, the more potential you have for happiness (Ps. 127:5), but only if you raise righteous children (Prov. 23:24). Otherwise, they will become a source of agony and heartbreak. Proverbs presents both sides of the picture. It talks about what happens when a child is not properly reared and given the right perspective on life. Children are a gift from God; they're meant for joy. However, if you try to rear children without Jesus Christ and without the guidance of the Spirit, and instead rear them on the world's psychology, you'll get just what we've got today—absolute chaos.

D. The Cause of the Present Chaos in Rearing Children

1. As seen by the Houston police department

The Houston police department years ago put out a leaflet called "How To Ruin Your Children." And it was guaranteed to be 99 percent effective. In part, this is what is said:

a) Principle #1—"Begin with infancy to give the child everything he wants."

b) Principle #2—"When he picks up bad words, laugh at him."

c) Principle #3—"Never give him any spiritual training. Let him wait until he's twenty-one years old, and then let him decide for himself."

d) Principle #4—"Avoid using the word 'wrong.' It may develop a serious guilt complex."

e) Principle #5—"Pick up everything he leaves lying around, so he will be experienced in throwing responsibility on everybody else."

2. As seen by a Christian psychiatrist

Christian psychiatrist Dr. Paul D. Meier, in his book *Christian Child-Rearing and Personality Development* ([Grand Rapids: Baker, 1977], pp. 49-79), facetiously discusses the tragedy of children raised without proper divine standards. He does it by showing steps to raising certain types of children.

a) How to develop a drug addict or alcoholic

   (1) "Spoil him; give him everything he wants if you can afford it."

   (2) "When he does wrong, you may nag him, but never spank him."

   (3) "Foster his dependence on you, so drugs or alcohol can replace you when he is older."

   (4) "Protect him from your husband and from those mean teachers who threaten to spank him from time to time. Sue them if you wish."

   (5) "Make all of his decisions for him, since you are a lot older and wiser than he is. He might make mistakes and learn from them if you don't."

   (6) "Criticize his father openly, so your son can lose his own self-respect and confidence."

   (7) "Always bail him out of trouble so he will like you. Besides, he might harm your reputation if he gets a police record. Never let him suffer the consequences of his own behavior."

   (8) "Always step in and solve his problems for him so he can depend on you and run to you when the going gets tough. Then when he is older and still hasn't learned how to solve his own problems, he can continue to run from them through heroin or alcohol."

(9) "Just to play it safe, be sure to dominate your husband and drive him to drink too, if you can."

(10) "Take lots of prescription drugs yourself, so that taking non-prescription drugs won't be a major step for him."

b) How to develop a homosexual

(1) "Start out by using the ten easy steps followed by the alcoholic's mother."

(2) "Show love for your son by protecting him very carefully. Don't let him play football or baseball with the other boys—he might get hurt! Don't let him be a newspaper boy or patrol boy; he might catch pneumonia out in the bad weather."

(3) "Be sure he spends a lot of time with you and little with his father (or any other adult males)."

c) How to develop a sociopathic criminal

(1) "As usual, start with the ten easy steps the alcoholic's mother uses, with the following exceptions and additions:"

(2) "Never spank your child. Physical punishment is a thing of the past. In fact, spanking is now considered immoral and is even against the law in Sweden."

(3) "Let your child express himself any way he feels. He'll learn from your example how to behave —he doesn't need any discipline."

(4) "Don't run his life; let him run yours. Let him manipulate you and play on your guilt if he doesn't get his own way."

(5) "Don't enforce the household rules—if there are any. That way he'll be able to choose which laws of society he will break when he is older, and he

won't fear the consequences, since he has never suffered any."

(6) "Don't bother him with chores. Do all of his chores for him. Then he can be irresponsible when he is older and always blame others when his responsibilities don't get done right."

(7) "Be sure to give in when he throws a temper tantrum. He might hit you if you don't. Don't ever cross him when he is angry."

(8) "It will help if you choose to believe his lies. You may even want to tell a few yourself."

(9) "Criticize others openly and routinely so he will realize that he is better than everyone else."

(10) "Give him a big allowance and don't make him do anything for it. He may get the idea that he'll have to work for a living later on if you make him work for it. If he does anything worthwhile around the house, be sure to pay him richly for each and every good deed. You wouldn't want him to think that a feeling of responsibility is its own reward."

d) How to develop a hysterical daughter

(1) "Use the same ten easy steps the alcoholic's mother used, point by point; but in addition do the following:"

(2) "Spoil her; always let her get her way, especially if she pouts or cries."

(3) "Always praise her for her looks, never for her character. Put a mirror on every wall, so she can continually admire herself."

(4) "Whenever she runs away—and she'll probably do this frequently—be sure to run after her and

apologize for not letting her have her own way in the first place."

(5) "Encourage her to become a movie star. By now she is so dramatic that acting would be quite natural for her."

(6) "Get divorced and remarried two or three times so she can learn what you already know: that all men are good-for-nothings, but you might as well live with one anyway."

e) How to develop an adult schizophrenic

Be sure you show no affection and be a weak father or mother.

f) How to develop an obsessive child

This kind of child is so rigid and inhibited that he's afraid of everything. Be sure to be critical, snobbish, domineering, and legalistic.

g) How to develop an accident-prone child

Parents should fight with each other constantly and blame the child for the fight so the child will go out and get hurt to punish himself. Or just ignore the child all the time so the child will get hurt to get attention. Or just overreact every time he scratches his finger.

h) How to develop an obese child

Feed him a lot of food and leave him home alone all the time so he has nothing to do but eat. Also make sure he has little regard for his father.

i) How to develop a hyperkinetic child

Don't ever spank the child; just nag him. Also make sure the father is always gone.

Why am I including all that? Because our society is full of those kinds of people. Where are they coming from? They come from families that are not responding to the divine principles God wants families to live by. No wonder 70 percent of the parents surveyed said if they had to do it over again, they wouldn't have any children. Who wants children with all the above problems? God intended for children to be a joy to their parents, but that will happen only when they are raised according to God's principles. Unfortunately, in our society, many children become nothing but a heartache.

3. As seen by the Minnesota Crime Commission

The Minnesota Crime Commission said this: "Every baby starts life as a little savage. He is completely selfish and self-centered. He wants what he wants when he wants it; his bottle, his mother's attention, his playmate's toys, his uncle's watch. Deny him these once, and he seethes with rage and aggressiveness which would be murderous were he not so helpless. He's dirty, he has no morals, no knowledge, no developed skills. This means that all children, not just certain children, all children are born delinquent. If permitted to continue in their self-impulsive actions to satisfy each want, every child would grow up a criminal, a killer, and a rapist."

That's human depravity. Just do nothing with your children, and that's what you're going to get. If you just let a child go his own way, make no consequences for his misbehavior, let him run his own life, and give him liberation, society will not want to live with what it's going to get.

Parents, if we don't work with our children to make them obedient, we're going to have the pain that the world has. It's not easy, but I know one thing: we must teach them to obey. And the only way you'll ever teach a child to obey is to make him pay the consequences for misbehavior. If you don't do that, your children will be a grief to you.

The Effects of a Disobedient Child

If you have a disobedient child, Proverbs says he will be:

1. A grief to his mother (10:1; 17:25)
2. A rebel to his father (15:5)
3. A sorrow to his father (17:21, 25)
4. A disaster to his father (19:13)
5. A disgrace to his parents (19:26)
6. A user of his parents (28:24)

That is summed up in Proverbs 29:15, which says, "The rod [what you do] and reproof [what you say] give wisdom, but a child left to himself bringeth his mother to shame." Do you want to have shame on your hands? Do you want to have a disaster on your hands? Just don't do anything, and that's what you'll have.

Review

I. THE SUBMISSION OF THE CHILD (vv. 1-3; see pp. 111-19)

Lesson

II. THE SUBMISSION OF THE PARENTS (v. 4)

"And, ye fathers, provoke not your children to wrath, but bring them up in the nurture and admonition of the Lord."

This is the top side of the authority/submission standard that upholds the family. Parents are to lead and rule but are also to submit to their children with loving, spiritual authority that does not abuse them.

The Power of the Father in Paul's Day

In Paul's day, certain attitudes existed that made life perilous for children. One of those was a Roman law called the *patria potestas*, which literally meant "the father's power." This particular law allowed the father to have absolute power over his family. He could sell them all as slaves; he could make them work in his fields in chains; and he could even take the law into his own hands and punish any member of his family as severely as he wanted, even to the point of inflicting the death penalty. And he had that power as long as he lived. When a child was born, for example, the child was taken and placed between the feet of the father. If the father reached down and picked up the child, the child stayed in the home. But if the father turned and walked away, the child was literally thrown away.

A letter of 1 B.C. from a man named Hilarion to his wife, Alis, gives us some insight into how children were viewed. It says, "Hilarion to Alis his wife, heartiest greetings. Know that we are still, even now, in Alexandria. Do not worry if when all others return, I remain in Alexandria. I beg and beseech you to take care of the little child, and as soon as we receive wages, I will send them to you. If —good luck to you—you have another child, if it is a boy, let it live; if it is a girl, expose it" (Papyri Oxyrhynchus IV, 744).

Seneca, a philosopher during the Roman Empire, said, "We slaughter a fierce ox, we strangle a mad dog, we plunge a knife into a sick cow, and children who are born weakly and deformed, we drown."

When children were thrown out by their parents, they would often be taken, if they were still alive, and left in the forum. People would then come by at night and collect the boys to make them slaves and the girls to raise as prostitutes.

So Paul was speaking to a world where the children were severely abused. The parent-child relationship was as sick as it is in our society—and, by the way, not much worse.

A. The Parents Identified

"Ye fathers."

The Greek word used here for "fathers" is *pateres*. It's usually the word for the male head of the family but sometimes is used to speak of the parents, encompassing both the mother and father. For example, in Hebrews 11:23 we read: "By faith Moses, when he was born, was hidden

134

three months by his parents [Gk., *pateres*], because they saw he was a beautiful child, and they were not afraid of the king's commandment." Here *pateres* refers to parents. The reason Ephesians 6:4 uses the male term is that the man is the head of the family, but the Greek term includes the mother. So I believe Paul is calling out to both parents, saying, "You can't just leave your child to develop on his own. You are the key to that child's life. Depravity will only continue unless he is broken by accountability and a loving environment of discipline." Children have to be cared for. They are mentally, physically, socially, and spiritually inadequate (see pp. 114-15). They need to grow in wisdom and stature and in favor with men and God (Luke 2:52).

How to Prevent Juvenile Delinquency

In a study conducted several years ago, sociologists Sheldon and Eleanor Glueck of Harvard University tried to identify the crucial factors in delinquency (*Unraveling Juvenile Delinquency* [Cambridge, Mass.: Harvard U., 1950], pp. 257-71). They developed a test by which they could predict the future delinquency of children five or six years old. Their follow-up tests four years later proved to be 90 percent accurate. They determined that the four necessary factors to prevent delinquency are:

1. The father's discipline

   Discipline must be firm and consistent.

2. The mother's supervision

   A mother must know where her children are and what they're doing at all times and be with them as much as possible.

3. The father and mother's affection

   Children need to see love demonstrated between the father and mother and have it physically demonstrated to them.

4. The family's cohesiveness

   The family must spend time together.

The Key to Right Parent-Child Relationships

Dr. Paul D. Meier (*Christian Child-Rearing and Personality Development*, pp. 81-82) sums up the key to right parent-child relationships in five things.

1. Love

   "Parents should have genuine love for each other and for their children."

2. Discipline

3. Consistency

   "Both parents should stick together, using the same rules and consistently enforcing those rules so that what a child gets away with on some occasions is not the cause for which he is capriciously punished at another time."

4. An example

   "In healthy families, the parents don't expect the children to live up to standards they themselves don't keep. Parents should expect their children to live up to the standards they themselves observe."

5. A man at the head of the home

   "The vast majority of neurotics, both children and adults, grew up in homes where there was no father or the father was absent or weak, and the mother was domineering."

What Meier is saying is that you must have the right role of both the father and the mother in order to insure the child's success in fulfilling God's pattern.

   B. The Parents Instructed

      1. The negative

         "Provoke not your children to wrath."

The word *provoke* means "to irritate" or "to make mad or angry." Sometimes it refers to a lashing, open rebellion, and sometimes it refers to an internal smoldering. But a parent, first of all, is not to provoke his child to wrath. How do you make your children angry? How do you provoke a child to become unruly, rebellious, or smoldering? Let me give you some suggestions.

a) Overprotection

Smother them, fence them in, never trust them, and always wonder whether they're telling you the truth. Never give them an opportunity to develop independence. In their environment, where everyone else takes certain risks and has certain opportunities, if they are compressed into a confined area, they'll begin to resent you and become angry. Parents, your children are people, and little by little they need to face the world and learn how to deal with it.

b) Favoritism

Prefer one child over another. Isaac favored Esau over Jacob, and Rebekah favored Jacob over Esau—you may know what terrible agony that caused. Don't ever compare a child with his siblings. You'll discourage him, make him angry, and break his spirit. Don't say things such as "Why can't you be bright like your sister? You always get C's and she gets A's" or "I never have to tell him twice to do anything" or "Why don't you act like your brother?" or "I only wanted two kids; why did you have to come along?" If you want to destroy your child, just make him feel inferior to everyone else in the family. You can test for this problem easily: ask your children how they feel about each other, and find out if they have preferences toward each other. If they do, they've probably picked them up from you.

c) Pushing achievement

Shove your child so hard to fulfill the goals you never accomplished that you destroy him. You can push so much that the child will have absolutely no sense of fulfillment; nothing is ever enough. Many parents pressure their children to excel in school, sports, or other activities, and it causes them to become bitter.

d) Discouragement

Provoke your child to wrath by discouraging him. That occurs if he's never given approval, reward, or honor; and if all you ever do is tell him what's bad, not what's good. I believe, in my own life, for every time I tell my child about something he's done wrong, I ought to equalize it by telling him something he's done right. Now, sometimes you have to look hard and be creative, but find something to praise him for. A child responds just as you do to reward, encouragement, and approval.

e) Failure to make sacrifices

Make them feel like an intrusion in your life. Childen are sensitive. They know what you mean when you say, "Well, we'd love to go with you, but we've got these kids, and we can't get anyone to stay with them. It's this way all the time," or, "Well, we'd like to get away, but what are we going to do with them?" If you make them feel unwanted and let them know there are many things that you'd like to do but can't because they're around, they'll soon begin to resent you.

f) Failure to allow for childishness

Make sure if they do anything that isn't adult, mature, and intellectual that you put them down for it. Don't let them say stupid or silly things. Make sure everything they do is always perfect. If you do that, you'll provoke them for sure. But on the other hand, it's exciting to just let them say what they want —even if it's dumb. Don't laugh then; laugh later if you have to laugh. Let them grow and present their ridiculous ideas.

g) Neglect

Neglect them. David neglected Absalom, and Absalom became the greatest heartbreak of David's life. You can't neglect your children and win. A friend of mine had a ministry traveling all over the country speaking to young people's groups. One day he overheard his little boy talking across the fence to the boy next door. "Hey, can you play catch?" his son asked. His playmate replied, "Naw, I'm going to play catch with my dad." Then the preacher heard his son say, "Oh, my dad doesn't have time to play with me. He's too busy playing with other people's kids." Needless to say, my friend changed his ministry. Don't ever be too busy.

h) Withdrawing love

Tell them you don't love them anymore. That is probably the fastest way to make a child insecure. Don't ever withdraw love as a punishment. You do that when you say, "Daddy won't like you if you do that." God never stops loving His children. Your child needs to know that you will never stop loving him.

i) Bitter words and cruel physical punishment

Take your anger out on your children. I don't know what causes men to batter children, but we all need to be careful; children are fragile. Fathers, don't shove your weight around and use your superior strength. That will provoke your children to wrath. Not only can children be battered physically, but they also can be devastated verbally. Parents are more erudite and sarcastic than children, and they can destroy and discourage a child through their verbal barrage. I'm always amazed to hear the things we say to our children that we would never say to an adult for fear of our reputation.

Don't provoke your children to wrath.

2. The positive

"Bring them up in the nurture and admonition of the Lord."

a) "Nurture"

This is the Greek word *paideia* and means "training, learning, instruction." This word is used in Hebrews 12:5, 7-8, 11 and is translated "discipline" or "chastening." There must be rules and regulations that lead to reward or punishment. The child is rewarded for keeping the rule and punished for breaking it. To nurture, then, is to train by rules and regulations enforced by rewards and punishments. And, of course, always in a context of love.

Advice from a Mother of Nineteen Children

Susanna Wesley, the mother of nineteen children, including John and Charles Wesley, wrote these words: "The parent who studies to subdue [self-will] in his child works together with God in the renewing and saving of a soul. The parent who indulges it does the Devil's work; makes religion impracticable, salvation unattainable, and [damns] his child, body, and soul for ever" (*Susanna: Mother of the Wesleys* [New York: Abingdon, 1968], pp. 59-60).

b) "Admonition"

Admonition is not what you do but what you say to a child. It is counsel. The word translated "admonition" is the Greek word *nouthesia* and means "verbal instruction with a view to correct." For example, it's saying, "If you keep doing that, you're going to run into problems," or, "I've got to counsel you about that." Throughout Proverbs we read that a wise son hears the counsel of his father and mother. That is admonition.

So on the one hand it's, "Do what I tell you," but on the other hand it's, "Listen to what I say." Nurture is correction; admonition is counsel. It's a tremendous task, and the end product is righteousness. If you want a righteous child, it has to come from what you teach him to do and what you tell him to do.

God wants to make our families into all they can be, and He wants to keep us from getting pressed into the mold of the world. Wouldn't it be great if Christian families didn't fall apart? Wouldn't it be great if Christian marriages stayed together? Wouldn't it be fantastic if we had children who were happy and homes that were Christ-centered, all things coming to pass as God designed them? It's possible! And if that ever happened, the world would take notice of us—and Christ.

Would You Do It Any Differently?

One father said, "My family's all grown, and the kids are all gone. But if I had to do it all over again, this is what I'd do:

1. I would love my wife more in front of my children.
2. I would laugh with my children more—at our mistakes and our joys.
3. I would listen more, even to the littlest child.
4. I would be more honest about my own weaknesses, never pretending perfection.
5. I would pray differently for my family—instead of focusing on them, I'd focus on me.
6. I would do more things together with my children.
7. I would encourage them more and bestow more praise.
8. I would pay more attention to little things, like deeds and words of thoughtfulness.
9. And then, finally, if I had to do it all over again, I would share God more intimately with my family; every ordinary thing that happened in every ordinary day I would use to direct them to God."

Focusing on the Facts

1. How does God call us to be different from the world in Ephesians (see p. 124)?

141

2. How did God expect Israel to be separate from the world (Lev. 18:3-5, 24-26; see pp. 124-25)?
3. What must we understand and begin to put into practice before we can pass on our Christian faith to the next generation (see p. 125)?
4. Cite evidence to show that much of society fails to see the value of children (see p. 126).
5. Show that God gives children as a gift to be enjoyed (see pp. 126-27).
6. When can children become a source of heartbreak and pain (see p. 127)?
7. List some things parents do that can cause their children to become drug addicts or alcoholics (see pp. 128-29).
8. What can the overprotection of a mother and the lack of normal male role-models lead a boy to become (see p. 129)?
9. How are criminals often produced (see pp. 129-30)?
10. What types of parental reactions can foster an accident-prone child (see p. 131)?
11. What should parents do to ensure that their child doesn't grow up to become a social misfit? What is the only way they can teach a child to obey (see p. 132)?
12. How are parents to submit to their children (Eph. 6:4; see p. 133)?
13. Describe the attitudes toward children in Paul's day (see p. 133-34).
14. What four factors are necessary for the prevention of juvenile delinquency (see p. 135)?
15. What does Paul instruct parents not to do in Ephesians 6:4? Explain (see p. 137).
16. Explain why it is important that children not be overprotected (see p. 137).
17. What must parents do to prevent their children from being discouraged when they have done something wrong (see p. 138)?
18. What made David's son Absalom become one of David's greatest heartbreaks (see p. 139)?
19. Why should parents not withdraw love as a punishment (see p. 139)?
20. What does it mean to nurture a child? Compare that with admonishing a child (see pp. 140-41).

Pondering the Principles

1. Parents, carefully review the lists of things on pages 128-31 that can contribute to a child's delinquency. Are you doing any of those things? I hope you are providing proper guidance for your children. However, do you see anything you may have overlooked? If so, talk it over with your spouse and plan a strategy for strengthening that area of weakness. Quickly seek to rectify any mistakes while your children's personalities are still easy to shape. If your child is older and you are now reaping the discouraging rewards of having neglected him, don't give up. Be firm and consistent with him, offering a loving family atmosphere that will be a guiding influence during the challenges of adolescence.

2. Do you recognize a need in your church for instruction on being good parents? Pray and plan with your church leaders on how that need can be met. Consider using a Christian film series on the family as a way of ministering to neighbors and friends who could benefit from instruction that encourages them to take a more active and biblical role in raising their children.

3. Do you love each of your children equally even though they have different personalities and abilities? Have you given them guidelines for what is right and wrong, and do you follow through with consistent and fair discipline or positive reinforcement when appropriate? Do you openly show affection to your spouse and enjoy each other's company when you spend time together? Do you set a consistent example that your children can respect and imitate? Do you provide sufficient supervision balanced with growing freedom and trust as your children mature? Is the principle of authority and submission in a context of love evident in your lives as parents? These elements are basic to a healthy family. If any of them are lacking, you need to begin implementing them today.

4. All of us have regretted something. Consider the list of things a father wishes he had done differently (p. 141). What advice of his can you begin heeding now—while there is still time?

Scripture Index